Editor
Lorin Klistoff, M.A.

Editorial Manager
Karen Goldfluss, M.S. Ed.

Editor in Chief
Sharon Coan, M.S. Ed.

Cover Artist
Sue Fullam

Art Coordinator
Cheri Macoubrie Wilson

Creative Director
Elayne Roberts

Imaging
James Edward Grace

Product Manager
Phil Garcia

Publishers
Rachelle Cracchiolo, M.S. Ed.
Mary Dupuy Smith, M.S. Ed.

STANDARDIZED TEST PRACTICE FOR 4TH GRADE

PROPERTY OF
Ms. L. Shiwlochan

D1097265

Author

Charles J. Shields

Teacher Created Materials, Inc.
6421 Industry Way
Westminster, CA 92683
www.teachercreated.com

©1999 Teacher Created Materials, Inc.
Reprinted, 2000

ISBN-1-57690-679-5

Made in U.S.A.

Table of Contents

Introduction

You have undoubtedly given plenty of tests during your years of teaching—unit tests, pop quizzes, final exams, and yes, standardized tests. As a professional educator, you know that standardized tests have taken on an importance greater than any of the others.

No one who understands children and the nature of learning would argue that a standardized test provides a measure of a child's understanding, a teacher's effectiveness, or a school's performance. It is a statistical snapshot of a group of children on a particular day. And there is no "generic child." Take a look at a girl named Joanna, for instance. Reluctant to speak during discussions or participate in group work, she's a whiz at taking tests and scores high on formal tests. However, Dion, in the seat beside her, is creative but impulsive. He dawdles during timed tests and sometimes fills in the wrong answer section. His score? It is no more a true indication of his ability than his doodles of motorcycle-riding monsters in the margins of his papers. You are probably thinking of a Joanna or a Dion in your class right now.

However, schools must be accountable to their communities. Moreover, issues of equity and opportunity for children require that some method of checking all students' progress as objectively as possible be administered annually or even semi-annually. As a result, at the insistence of parents, school boards, state legislatures, and national commissions, standardized tests and their results are receiving more attention than at any other time during the last 35 years.

The purpose of this book is to help you and your students get better results on standardized tests. The exercises are grade-specific and based on the most recent versions of these testing instruments:

The California Achievement Tests
The Iowa Tests of Basic Skills
The Comprehensive Tests of Basic Skills
The Stanford Achievement Tests
The Metropolitan Achievement Tests
The Texas Assessment of Academic Skills

Exercise materials designed for this book reflect skills from curricula, grade-level tests, and test taking from the California Academic Standards Commission, the New York State Testing Program for Elementary and Intermediate Grades, the Texas Essential Knowledge and Skills program, and the Board of Education for the Commonwealth of Virginia. Your students can expect to meet again on widely-used standardized tests most of the content in this book and the style in which questions are posed.

About the Practice Tests

You will notice several things right away about the exercises.

1. The tests are arranged by curricular topics: punctuation, reading comprehension, or adding decimals, for example.

2. The exercises are short enough that you can integrate them into your teaching day. If you spend 20 minutes daily on test taking over several weeks as you approach a test date, your students will build confidence and increase their knowledge base in preparation for the actual test. Becoming familiar with testing formats and practicing on sample questions is one of the most effective ways to improve scores.

3. Examples of student-constructed responses to problems and questions have been included. Students must write, draw, or show their work to get credit for their answers.

Each section of the book—Language Arts, Mathematics, Science, Social Studies—begins with a short lesson for students about answering the questions in that section. A list of test-taking tips appears at the end of the lesson. It would be a good idea to have your students take turns reading portions of the lesson aloud so you can emphasize key suggestions.

Ways to Increase Students' Confidence

- Downplay the importance of how many right answers versus how many wrong answers your students give. These exercises generally have the same purpose as drills in sports—to improve players' ability through regular practice. Fill the role of coach as students learn to hit the long ball.

- Give credit for reasonable answers. Encourage students to explain why they answered as they did. Praise thoughtfulness and good guesses. Surprise them by giving partial credit because their logic is persuasive. On some state-designed tests, credit is given for "almost right" answers.

- Promote in your classroom a positive, relaxed feeling about test taking. It might be wise, for example, to put off administering a planned practice from this booklet if your students are anxious or feeling overwhelmed about something. Use a little psychology in strengthening the association in their minds between test taking and opportunities to feel pleased about oneself.

The following pages provide a list of the basic skills embedded in the tests in this book.

Language Arts

Reading Comprehension
Author's Purpose
Cause and Effect
Compare and Contrast
Conflict
Fact Versus Opinion
Fiction
Figurative Language
Inferences
Main Ideas
Nonfiction
Plot
Poetry
Point of View
Prediction
Reality Versus Fantasy
Research
Rhyming
Sequencing
Setting
Supporting Details
Topic Sentences

Vocabulary
Affixes
Antonyms
Multiple Meanings
Synonyms

Writing
Capitalization
Combining
Conjugation
Contractions
Editing
Elaborating
Paragraphing
Pronoun Referents
Punctuation

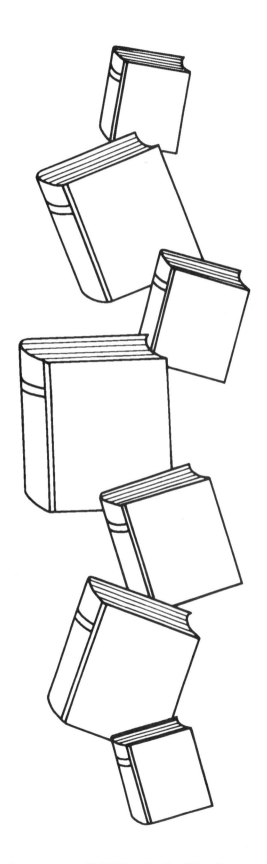

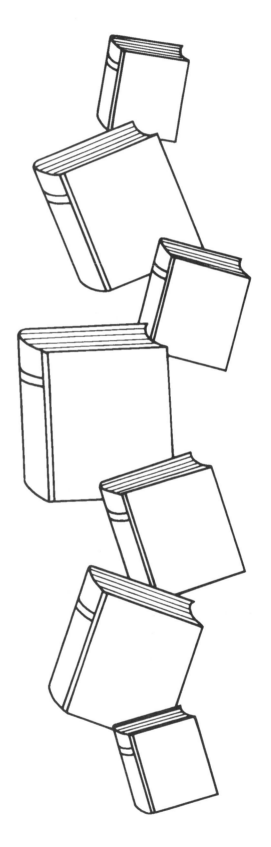

Mathematics *(cont.)*

Fractions *(cont.)*

Subtracting Like and Unlike Denominators

Subtracting Mixed Numerals

Geometry

Area

Basic Terms

Lines: Segments, Parallel, Intersecting

Perimeter

Points on a Number Line

Shapes and Angles

Vertices, Edges, Faces

Volume

Metric Units

Multiplication

Factors

One-Digit by One-Digit

Two-Digit by One-Digit

Two-Digit by Two-Digit

Three-Digit by One-Digit

Three-Digit by Two-Digit

Four-Digit by One-Digit

Greatest Common Factor

Least Common Multiple

Multiples of 10, 100, and 1,000

Problem Solving

Solving Word Problems

Multiplication and Division

Patterns

Representing in Picture, Word, and Number Form

Roman Numerals

Whole Numbers

Adding and Subtracting

Place Value

Prime Factorization

Prime Numbers

Rounding

Solving Word Problems

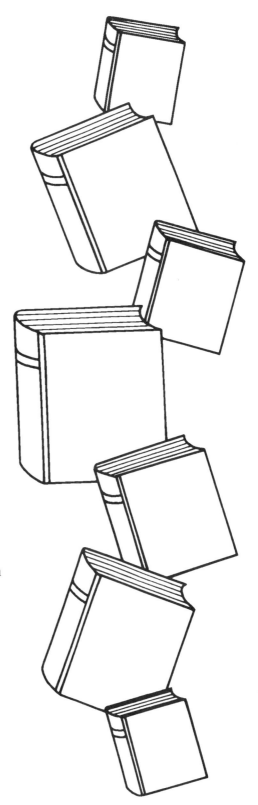

Science

Social Studies

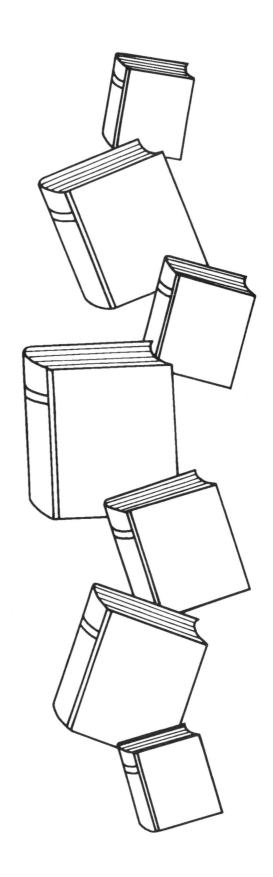

Why Take Tests?

The reason is that your teacher, your parents, and school leaders such as the principal all want to know more about what you're learning in school.

They can tell partly from your daily grades, from your reports, and from your work posted on the bulletin board in your classroom, but a test has its own, special purpose. The purpose of a test is to measure what you know and how you think.

There are several ways to do this. A test can be graded by

- how many right answers or how many wrong answers you get.

- how many questions you finish.

- how your score compares to the scores of other students at your school or to scores of other students from all over the United States!

Naturally, you might be asking yourself, "What difference does it make what score I get on a test?" The answer is the scores on tests make a difference to your school and how you are taught.

Here is an example. Imagine that your physical education teacher knows that by October, all fourth graders who are not physically challenged in any special way should be able to run around the school one time without stopping to rest.

She lines everyone up, says, "Ready, set, go!" and everyone starts to run. She writes down the time as each student crosses the finish line. That night, she studies all the finishing times, and she is surprised! The average time it took everyone to finish was longer than what she expected. In fact, a few students had trouble finishing at all, even though they tried their best. Why was the average finishing time longer? Were the students not ready to run that day? Did they not understand the right way to go around the school? Do they need more practice at running long distances? What can the teacher do, she wonders, to improve the students' finishing time?

That is what a test does; it gives teachers, parents, and school administrators clues about what the students can or cannot do and how to help them. Based on test results, a classroom teacher might focus more on teaching fractions, writing, or United States history, for instance. He or she might try putting students into small reading groups or allowing students to work on math problems in pairs.

As you can see, it is important that you try your best on a test. It makes a big difference between a score that shows what you really know and one that does not represent your ability and understanding. Turn to the next page to find out how you can "test your best."

Lesson 1: Marking Your Answers

The purpose of this lesson is to introduce you to the correct way to mark your answers on a standardized test.

A standardized test is one that is given to thousands and thousands of students. The writers of the questions try to be as fair as possible. After all, it wouldn't mean anything if all fourth-grade students took different kinds of tests—some easy, some hard. The results would be confusing and meaningless.

The scoring of standardized tests tries to be as fair as possible, too. It is done by a computer. However, for computer-scored tests, answer sheets must be marked the same way by all students. That is why everyone must use a pencil marked No. 2 and fill in the circles with dark marks.

Attention must also be paid to how a question is written. For example, a question on a standardized test might look like this:

Directions: Fill in the circle of your answer.

How do you write the plural of the word "mouse"?

mouses	mices	mice	meeses
○	○	○	○

You would fill in the circle under "mice." But what if the question were written this way?

Directions: Fill in the circle of your answer.

How do you write the plural of "house"?

(A) hice

(B) hices   Ⓐ   Ⓑ   Ⓒ   Ⓓ

(C) hoose

(D) houses

You would fill in the circle with D inside of it, not fill in the (D) before the word "houses." If you did that, the computer would mark your answer as incorrect. Unfortunately, the computer would have no way of determining that you knew the plural of house!

Lesson 1: Marking Your Answers *(cont.)*

Of course, you will not fill in answers as soon as you are handed a standardized test. The first thing you will do is put your name on the answer sheet. Here is an example:

Each filled-in circle stands for a letter in someone's name. Figure out the person's name by looking at the filled-in circles and then writing the letter of the circle in the empty box above the row. Notice that the person filled in blank circles for spaces anywhere in her name, including leftover spaces at the end. Circles must be filled in under every box.

Did you figure out the person's name?

Last Name   **First Name**

(Bubble answer grid with columns of circles labeled A through Z. Blank top-row circles are used for spaces. In the Last Name section the filled circles spell, reading down each column: L, O, C, K, S, followed by filled spaces. In the First Name section the filled circles spell: G, O, L, D, I, E, followed by filled spaces.)

Lesson 2: Minding the Minutes

The purpose of this lesson is to help you learn how to answer the most questions you can on a standardized test.

A standardized test is timed. It is another way of trying to make the test fair. It would not be fair to allow some students to spend an hour solving a dozen one-step math problems—which is much longer than necessary—and a second group of students to spend only fifteen minutes. Would it be clear who understood the problems better? No, it would not be a fair or an accurate measure of the students' abilities.

Keep in mind that you get credit for the number of questions you answer correctly. The more questions you answer correctly, the higher your score. Keeping this in mind, what do you think you should do when you have a limited amount of time to answer a lot of questions?

To answer this question, imagine what you would do in another situation. You are about to play a game outside. In this game, you have ten minutes to gather all the pieces of candy you can. The pieces have been hidden in the grass, in the bushes, and next to stones. Some of them are easy to see; some are well-hidden. Now, what would you do?

You would probably run around and pick up all the pieces you could see right away. If you still had time, you could go back and search for the pieces that are well-hidden. But remember—the idea is to get as many pieces of candy as you can. So go for the easy ones first!

Believe it or not, the same strategy works on a standardized test. See for yourself. Here are three math questions that you must finish with only one minute left on the test.

---

1. $\dfrac{2}{6}$

   $+ \dfrac{1}{6}$

   (A) $\frac{1}{6}$
   (B) $\frac{3}{12}$
   (C) $\frac{3}{6}$
   (D) 3
   (E) none of these

   Fill in the correct circle.

   Ⓐ Ⓑ Ⓒ Ⓓ Ⓔ

---

2. $\dfrac{?}{35} = \dfrac{2}{7}$

   (F) 7
   (G) 5
   (H) 10
   (J) 11
   (K) none of these

   Fill in the correct circle.

   Ⓕ Ⓖ Ⓗ Ⓙ Ⓚ

---

3. $\dfrac{3}{8} + \dfrac{1}{4} =$

   (A) $\frac{2}{4}$
   (B) $\frac{2}{8}$
   (C) $\frac{4}{12}$
   (D) $\frac{4}{8}$
   (E) none of these

   Fill in the correct circle.

   Ⓐ Ⓑ Ⓒ Ⓓ Ⓔ

Lesson 2: Minding the Minutes *(cont.)*

You might be able to answer all three problems on the previous page, but if you had to choose, which would you skip? You would probably not try problem 2 since it looks like it would take the longest amount of time to solve.

What if there are 25 math problems on one part of a test and you skipped six of them because they looked like they would take longer to solve? How do you remind yourself to go back? Put a little check mark on your answer sheet next to each problem you skipped. If there is time, you can go back and work on the harder problems.

Here is one more example in which you might have to skip questions on a test, but the choice is a little different. What if there are two reading passages on a test—one has four questions after it, and the other one has eight? You think you only have time to read one of the passages. Which one should you choose?

Choose the one with eight questions after it. Maybe you will only have time to answer six of the eight questions, but you will probably get more of them right than if you read the other passage, answered the four questions, and then were reading the second passage when you ran out of time.

Whenever you can, answer correctly as many questions as you can on a standardized test. That's the smart way to mind the minutes.

Lesson 3: Guessing Correctly

This lesson will explain to you that it is possible to answer a question correctly even if you're just guessing; the secret is narrowing your choices.

Sometimes you will be faced with a really difficult multiple-choice question. It might be that
- you do not understand the question very well.
- you do not understand the answer choices.
- you simply do not know the answer at all.

What should you do? Guess? Yes, you should guess. But you can increase the chance of choosing the correct answer by using a few strategies.

"Best-Guess" Strategies

1. **Always make sure to read all the choices.** Do not jump at the first one that looks like it might be right. Here is an example:

Which is the largest city?

(A) Los Angeles
(B) Detroit
(C) Atlanta
(D) New York

Fill in the correct circle.

Ⓐ Ⓑ Ⓒ Ⓓ

Lesson 3: Guessing Correctly *(cont.)*

"Best-Guess" Strategies *(cont.)*

Maybe you do not know which is the largest city, but you do know that (A) "Los Angeles" is bigger than (B) "Detroit," so you choose (A) "Los Angeles" and go on the next question. But wait! It is important to read all the choices. In fact, (D) "New York" is the largest city. You might have guessed between (A) "Los Angeles" or (D) "New York" if you had read all the possible answers. To be a good guesser, you must read every choice and think about each of them, one at a time. If you are the kind of tester who always reads all the choices before choosing one, then you are doing the right thing.

2. Eliminate the answer choices that are plainly wrong.

Here is an example of a social studies question you might find on a test. Choose the correct term.

How can the president stop a law that has been passed by Congress?

(A) politics

(B) capital

(C) veto

(D) arrest

Fill in the correct circle.

Ⓐ   Ⓑ   Ⓒ   Ⓓ

Think carefully about this situation. Choice (A) "politics" is something like "business" or "teaching"— it is a profession. How could it be used to stop anything? Next, (B) "capital" is usually a place, like a state capital. It could not be used to stop a process like passing a law. What about (D) "arrest"? People do get stopped when they are put "under arrest," but this is a law being talked about, not people, so (D) "arrest" is probably not the correct answer. That leaves (C) "veto" as the most likely choice, because each of the other choices does not quite fit for some reason. If you chose (C) "veto," you would be right.

3. Look carefully for clues about how the word is used.

On some tests, you might run across a reading passage that has vocabulary words that you do not know. Here is an example of such a reading passage.

In *The Goats* (1987), Brock Cole's first novel, Howie Mitchell and Laura Golden meet at Tall Pine, a summer camp. They recognize each other as outcasts. "I'm socially retarded for my age," Laura tells Howie. "Yeah. Me too," Howie replies. But deep down, neither of them believes those statements. When a cruel practical joke leaves them abandoned on an island, they seize the opportunity to test their self-reliance and independence. They escape from the island, steer clear of their camp, and make do for themselves. They remain on the run until they are confident they have new identities they can be proud of.

Based on the passage you read, what is the meaning of the word *self-reliance* in this passage?

(A) personal courage

(B) tools

(C) meanness

(D) depending on oneself

Fill in the correct circle.

Ⓐ   Ⓑ   Ⓒ   Ⓓ

Lesson 3: Guessing Correctly *(cont.)*

"Best-Guess" Strategies *(cont.)*

In this case, if you do not know the meaning of the word *self-reliance*, you need to look carefully for clues about how the word is used. The passage says Howie and Laura were abandoned on an island and used the "opportunity to test their self-reliance and courage." Why would they test their (C) "meanness" in such a situation? That does not make much sense. And nothing is said about them having (B) "tools." If they had tools, it would not have been a "cruel practical joke" to leave them abandoned on an island. "Tools" is not a good choice. They might have tested their (A) "personal courage," but the passage also said they "make do for themselves" which suggests (D) "depending on oneself." So both (A) and (D) are likely choices, but at least you have eliminated two of the four choices. Now you have a fifty-fifty chance of getting the answer correct. Which do you choose, (A) or (D)? The answer is (D) "depending on oneself."

4. **For a math problem, you can use estimating to help you when you are not sure of the answer.**

Now try this problem.

The choir practiced for $2\frac{3}{4}$ hours on Saturday and $3\frac{2}{3}$ hours on Sunday. How much was the total time?

(A) $4\frac{3}{4}$

(B) $5\frac{17}{12}$

(C) $5\frac{7}{8}$

(D) $6\frac{5}{12}$

Fill in the correct circle.

(A)   (B)   (C)   (D)

Maybe this problem gives you trouble because you have difficulty with fractions. Use estimation to help you make your best guess.

Looking at the whole numbers in the problem, the choir practiced 2 hours + 3 hours which totals 5 hours. Five is more than (A) $4\frac{3}{4}$ hours. You know that is true even without adding the fractions. (A) cannot be correct. Next, the mixed number (B) $5\frac{17}{12}$ is strange. Have you ever seen a mixed number in which the numerator of the fraction is larger than the denominator? (B) is probably not correct either. (C) $5\frac{7}{8}$ is a possibility, but look closely; 8 is not a common denominator of $\frac{3}{4}$ and $\frac{2}{3}$. How could you get an answer like (C) $5\frac{7}{8}$? That leaves (D) $6\frac{5}{12}$.

If you guessed (D) even without doing the problem, you would be right. You did some quick estimating to solve the problem.

Remember to use these four strategies:

- Make sure to read all the answer choices.
- Eliminate choices that are plainly wrong.
- Look for clues about how a word is used.
- Estimate the answer.
  You are sure to raise your test scores if you practice guessing correctly.

Introduction

The language arts section of standardized tests always involves a lot of reading. There are short questions, too, of course, but quite often you must read a paragraph or a long passage to answer the questions.

Here's the Idea

To answer your best on the language arts sections, you must be able to do the following:

1. Identify main ideas.
2. Recognize important details or clues.
3. Draw conclusions on your own.

Before we look at each of the three skills, read the following tips that apply to taking any test, whether it is in language arts, math, science, or social studies. These tips will be repeated because they are important!

Test-Taking Tips

- **Read directions carefully before marking any test questions**, even though you have done that kind of test before. You may think you already know what the directions say, but don't ignore them—read them over. If you do not understand the directions, raise your hand and ask for help. Although your teacher must read the directions exactly as they are written, the teacher can make sure you understand what the directions mean.

- **Follow instructions.** Pay close attention to the sample exercises. They will help you understand what the items on the test will be like and how to mark your answer sheet properly.

- **Read the entire question and all the answer choices.** Do not stop reading when you have found a correct answer. Choices D or E may read "B and D" or "all of the above." On some tests, two answers are both correct. You need to read all the answer choices before marking your answer.

- **For long reading passages, read the questions first so you know what to look for.** If you read the questions first, you will find information in the passage that answers the questions.

- **Remember that taking a test is not a race!** There are no prizes for finishing first. Use all of the time provided for the test. If you have time left over, check your answers.

Try and Discuss

Now let's discuss the same three skills (*identifying main ideas*, *recognizing important details or clues*, and *drawing conclusions on your own*) for language arts tests.

Take a look at the question below.

Which one names the whole group?

    (A) Earth

    (B) Mercury

    (C) Pluto

    (D) solar system

    (E) orbits

Fill in the correct circle.

Ⓐ   Ⓑ   Ⓒ   Ⓓ   Ⓔ

One of these words includes all of the others. It is (D) "solar system." The planets—Earth, Mercury, and Pluto—are all part of the solar system, and all the planets travel in an orbit in the solar system.

The main idea of a paragraph is just like that—it is an idea that names all of the other ideas in the paragraph by making them one group. You will be asked to identify main ideas on language arts tests. You also may be asked, "What would be a good title for this?" which is another way of asking, "What is the main idea?"

This time, look at the list of words below and decide what is the main idea of this group. (**Hint: The main idea is not mentioned!**)

What is the main idea that connects these things?

    (A) candles

    (B) games

    (C) ice cream

    (D) cake

    (E) gifts

    (F) guests

What do you think? _____

Think of a main idea that would include all of these things. You might come to the conclusion that the answer is a *birthday party*. In this case, you have to draw your own conclusion. In other words, you have to make a good guess at what the main idea is, even though it does not appear in words.

Sometimes the main idea of a paragraph is given in words directly—as in the solar system example above—but sometimes the main idea is only suggested, as in the birthday party example.

Try and Discuss *(cont.)*

Now take a look at an actual paragraph. You decide what the main idea is.

> ### Welcome Pool Members!
>
> Welcome to the Millertown pool, created by the parks and recreation department for all residents of Millertown. Please keep in mind that many people use the pool in the summer and that rules must be followed. First, running, pushing, or shoving is never allowed. Walk slowly. Second, do not jump from the side of the pool. You might land on someone and hurt the person. Use the diving board for jumping instead. Third, it is good to have fun in the pool, but no rough play is permitted. If the lifeguard sees dangerous behavior, the swimmers will be told to stop immediately. Enjoy yourself while you're here—Millertown pool is for everyone!

The main idea of this paragraph is

    (A) summer.

    (B) swimming.

    (C) pool safety.

    (D) having fun.

Fill in the correct circle.

Ⓐ   Ⓑ   Ⓒ   Ⓓ

This paragraph is an example of one of those times when you must both recognize important details or clues and draw conclusions on your own.

Eliminate choices by looking for details. For example, you might think that (A) "summer" is correct because, after all, people go to a pool in the summer. But look closely. How many details are about summer in the paragraph? The summer months are not mentioned; the temperature in the summertime is not mentioned. There are no details about summer.

How about choice (B) "swimming"? The paragraph is all about swimming or, at least, using the pool. But in fact, there are no details about how to swim or when to swim. Most of the details—"walk slowly" and "no rough play"—are about safety at the pool. So (C) "pool safety" is the correct answer. What about (D) "having fun"? Draw your own conclusion; see how many details about having fun you can find in the paragraph.

Tips That Help

Remember the following tips:

- The main idea in a paragraph covers all the other ideas in the paragraph or passage.
- Sometimes you must draw your own conclusion. Look for details that support your good guess about what the main idea is.

 Now try the practice tests. Follow the test directions and solve the sample problems to be sure you understand what to do on each test.

Directions: Fill in the answer circle for the correct way to divide the word in syllables.

Samples

A. (A) chi-mney
(B) chim-ney
(C) chimn-ey

B. (F) stopli-ght
(G) sto-plight
(H) stop-light

1. (A) eng-ine
(B) engin-e
(C) en-gine

2. (F) weath-er
(G) weat-her
(H) wea-ther

3. (A) ca-stle
(B) cas-tle
(C) cast-le

4. (F) qu-ickly
(G) quic-kly
(H) quick-ly

5. (A) cree-ping
(B) creep-ing
(C) cre-eping

6. (F) foo-tball
(G) footba-ll
(H) foot-ball

7. (A) a-round
(B) arou-nd
(C) aro-und

8. (F) su-nset
(G) suns-et
(H) sun-set

9. (A) extr-a
(B) ext-ra
(C) ex-tra

10. (F) doo-rbell
(G) doorb-ell
(H) door-bell

11. (A) tic-ket
(B) tick-et
(C) ti-cket

12. (F) benea-th
(G) ben-eath
(H) be-neath

➤ **STOP** ◄

Directions: Read the sentence carefully. Fill in the circle for any word that is misspelled. If all the words are correct, fill in the circle for "no mistake."

Samples

   A. The <u>sled</u> <u>bounced</u> down the hill to the edge of the <u>streem</u>.   <u>no mistake</u>
         A   B   C   D

   B. The <u>bus</u> <u>stopped</u> in front of the train <u>station</u>.   <u>no mistake</u>
         F   G   H   J

---

1. His <u>birthday</u> party is <u>planed</u> for <u>Wednesday</u>.   <u>no mistake</u>
      A   B   C   D

---

2. No one <u>new</u> who <u>shouted</u>, "<u>Batter</u> up!"   <u>no mistake</u>
         F   G   H   J

---

3. The mother cat <u>hid</u> the <u>kittens</u> under the <u>stares</u>.   <u>no mistake</u>
                 A   B   C   D

---

4. Don't tell Andrew <u>about</u> the <u>suprise</u> we <u>bought</u>.   <u>no mistake</u>
                     F   G   H   J

---

5. Pay <u>attenshion</u> to all <u>playground</u> <u>rules</u>, please.   <u>no mistake</u>
      A   B   C   D

---

6. Did you <u>believe</u> the <u>storey</u> about the <u>queen</u>?   <u>no mistake</u>
          F   G   H   J

---

7. The <u>roots</u> of trees <u>spread</u> out as wide as the <u>branches</u>.   <u>no mistake</u>
      A   B   C   D

---

8. The <u>general</u> gave a <u>comand</u>, and the soldiers <u>obeyed</u>.   <u>no mistake</u>
      F   G   H   J

---

9. The police <u>officer</u> directs <u>traffick</u> every day near the <u>bakery</u>.   <u>no mistake</u>
             A   B   C   D

---

10. Snow on the <u>mountain</u> melted, <u>filling</u> the lake in the <u>valley</u> below.   <u>no mistake</u>
               F   G   H   J

➤ **STOP** ◄

Directions: Look for a usage mistake in each item. In the rows below, fill in the answer circle for the line with the mistake. If you do not find a mistake, fill in the letter that matches with "no mistake."

Samples

A. (A) Tim went to the corner (B) to wait for the bus. He waves (C) as it approached. (D) no mistakes	**B.** (F) The river runs south for (G) hundreds of miles before (H) reaching the sea. (J) no mistakes

---

1. (A) Lupe opened the door of
   (B) the refrigerator hopefully,
   (C) but there were nothing inside.
   (D) no mistake

2. (F) It took Robert three hours
   (G) to rake them leaves up.
   (H) He finished at noon.
   (J) no mistake

3. (A) My mother gave us five
   (B) dollars for the carnival.
   (C) Me and Manny thanked her.
   (D) no mistake

4. (F) Kent found a field mouse
   (G) in his backyard. He brung
   (H) a drawing of it to school.
   (J) no mistake

5. (A) My sister hasn't never
   (B) gone to bed without saying
   (C) good night to all of us.
   (D) no mistake

6. (F) We is proud to be
   (G) representing our team
   (H) in the contest.
   (J) no mistake

7. (A) My sister Tasha she has
   (B) a game that's missing the
   (C) directions, so we pretend.
   (D) no mistake

8. (F) Marsha is the only student
   (G) in gym class who can do
   (H) nine pull-ups in a row.
   (J) no mistakes

9. (A) Mom wasn't feeling well.
   (B) Dad said him and me
   (C) would go shopping ourselves.
   (D) no mistakes

10. (F) My brother isn't in school
    (G) yet. He ask a lot of questions
    (H) about what it's like.
    (J) no mistake

➤ **STOP** ◄

Writing: Capitalization

Directions: Read each sentence. Choose the correct way to capitalize the word or group of words that go in the blank. Fill in the answer circle for your choice.

Samples

A. My favorite book is _____.
(A) *The Trumpeter swan*
(B) *the Trumpeter Swan*
(C) *The Trumpeter Swan*
(D) *the trumpeter swan*

B. Have you read the story _____?
(F) "the Lion and the Mouse"
(G) "the lion and the Mouse"
(H) "The lion and The Mouse"
(J) "The Lion and the Mouse"

---

1. I was in a parade on _____.

   (A) labor day

   (B) Labor day

   (C) Labor Day

   (D) labor Day

2. My aunt lives in _____.

   (F) Baltimore, Maryland

   (G) Baltimore, maryland

   (H) baltimore, maryland

   (J) baltimore, Maryland

3. The hurricane struck the coast of _____.

   (A) central America

   (B) Central america

   (C) Central America

   (D) central america

4. We explored a submarine at the _____.

   (F) Museum of science and Industry

   (G) Museum of Science and Industry

   (H) museum of science and Industry

   (J) museum of science and industry

5. *The Wizard of Oz* was written by _____.

   (A) l. Frank Baum

   (B) L. frank Baum

   (C) L. Frank baum

   (D) L. Frank Baum

6. Send the letter to _____.

   (F) mrs. Rose Miller

   (G) Mrs. Rose miller

   (H) mrs. rose miller

   (J) Mrs. Rose Miller

7. Chicago is a stop on the _____.

   (A) illinois central Railroad

   (B) Illinois central Railroad

   (C) Illinois Central Railroad

   (D) illinois central railroad

8. Thousands of people visit the _____.

   (F) grand Canyon

   (G) grand canyon

   (H) Grand canyon

   (J) Grand Canyon

➤ **STOP** ◄

Writing: Punctuation

Directions: Read the sentence, and check the punctuation. Fill in the answer circle for the punctuation that needs to be added. Fill in the circle for "none" if no other punctuation mark is needed.

Sample

A. I put my *books lunch, and calculator* in my backpack.

(A) .   (B) :   (C) ,   (D) ;   (E) none

---

1. "Marie!" Andrew yelled from the shore. *"Arent you cold?"*

   (A) '   (B) :   (C) !   (D) "   (E) none

---

2. Lupita, why don't you wait inside *for your ride*

   (F) ?   (G) ,   (H) "   (J) .   (K) none

---

3. James Hart Elementary School *has 267 students in six grades.*

   (A) :   (B) ,   (C) .   (D) ?   (E) none

---

4. Have you ever stood at the top of *the Statue of Libertys torch* and seen the view?

   (F) Liberty's   (G) Libertys's   (H) Libertie's   (J) Libertys'   (K) none

---

5. The surprise attack on Pearl Harbor *was December 7 1941.*

   (A) ,   (B) !   (C) "   (D) :   (E) none

---

6. "When Grandpa stops by, *well tell him the news,"* Ian said.

   (F) "   (G) .   (H) '   (J) ;   (K) none

---

7. Who wants this last piece *of French silk pie*

   (A) "   (B) .   (C) !   (D) ?   (E) none

---

8. *I cant' tell if it's Dave's* baseball glove or not.

   (F) can't   (G) ca'nt   (H) its   (J) Daves'   (K) none

➤ **STOP** ◄

Writing: Sentences

Directions: Answer the questions in italics.

1. Combine these sentences. "One-third of Earth's surface is desert. It is land with little rainfall." *Which sounds best?*

    (A) Little rain falls on the desert.

    (B) One-third of Earth's surface is desert, where there is little rainfall.

    (C) One-third of Earth gets little rainfall, the desert.

    (D) Little rainfall, the desert covers one-third of Earth's surface.

2. Combine these sentences. "Deserts are always dry. They may be hot. They may be cold." *Which sounds best?*

    (F) Hot and cold, deserts are dry.

    (G) Deserts are always dry, but they may be hot or cold.

    (H) Hot deserts or cold deserts, but always dry.

    (J) They are always dry. Deserts are hot or cold.

3. Combine these sentences. "Deserts make good laboratories. Scientists can study well-preserved fossils there. It's because deserts are so dry." *Which sounds best?*

    (A) Dry deserts make good laboratories for studying well-preserved fossils.

    (B) Well-preserved fossils are in deserts, which are so dry, scientists can study them.

    (C) Because deserts are so dry, they make good laboratories for scientists studying well-preserved fossils.

    (D) Why do scientists study fossils in the desert? It's because they are so dry.

4. "Very little vegetation lives in the desert." *What is the subject of the sentence?*

    (F) desert

    (G) vegetation

    (H) very little

    (J) lives

5. "Deserts can be easily damaged, even though they are harsh environments." *What is the subject of the sentence?*

    (A) they

    (B) environments

    (C) deserts

    (D) damaged

➤ **STOP** ◄

Directions: Read the sentences below, and answer the question.

The principal of your school is thinking about putting a fast-food counter in the cafeteria, run by a major fast-food restaurant chain. These lunches would cost a little more than school lunches. Do you think this is a good idea?

Write a paragraph explaining your reasons.

_____

_____

_____

_____

_____

_____

_____

_____

_____

_____

_____

_____

_____

_____

_____

_____

_____

_____

Teacher Note: Student responses are to be evaluated by the teacher.

➤ STOP ◄

Vocabulary: Multiple Meanings

Directions: Read the pair of word meanings. Look for the word that fits both meanings. Mark the answer space for your choice.

Samples

   A. a kind of transportation and to make an animal obey

       (A) plane   (B) steps   (C) train   (D) show

   B. to bend at the waist and used with an arrow

       (F) point   (G) bow   (H) stoop   (J) notch

1. the center of a hurricane and used to see with

    (A) light   (B) cloudless   (C) pupil   (D) eye

2. a piece of wood and to prevent

    (F) splinter   (G) stop   (H) block   (J) knot

3. at the tip of your finger and used by carpenters

    (A) cuticle   (B) end   (C) nail   (D) clipper

4. a support for a sign and to hang a sign

    (F) bar   (G) post   (H) tape   (J) hook

5. to examine closely and a place to read quietly

    (A) observatory (B) study   (C) peer   (D) library

6. weapons and part of the human body

    (F) nuclear   (G) arms   (H) mind   (J) tank

➤ **STOP** ◄

Vocabulary: Affixes

Directions: Read each pair of words, and look for the word or words that best tell the meaning of the underlined affix. Fill in the answer circle for your choice.

Samples

A. <u>bi</u>cycle   <u>bi</u>noculars
- (A) away
- (B) not
- (C) two
- (D) between

B. hero<u>ic</u>   acid<u>ic</u>
- (F) some
- (G) like
- (H) in the direction of
- (J) one who

1. <u>mis</u>print   <u>mis</u>use
- (A) under
- (B) over
- (C) between
- (D) incorrect

5. care<u>less</u>   fear<u>less</u>
- (A) below
- (B) without
- (C) like
- (D) opposite from

2. <u>trans</u>mit   <u>trans</u>portation
- (F) between
- (G) after
- (H) across
- (J) in place of

6. froz<u>en</u>   wood<u>en</u>
- (F) able to
- (G) made of
- (H) away from
- (J) with

3. <u>sub</u>merge   <u>sub</u>soil
- (A) across
- (B) under
- (C) less
- (D) greater

7. music<u>ian</u>   beautic<u>ian</u>
- (A) in the manner of
- (B) in place of
- (C) having a certain skill
- (D) less

4. <u>non</u>toxic   <u>non</u>sense
- (F) more
- (G) less
- (H) not
- (J) under

8. teach<u>er</u>   bak<u>er</u>
- (F) able to
- (G) like
- (H) with
- (J) one who

➢ **STOP** ◅

Vocabulary: Synonyms and Antonyms

Directions: Read the underlined word in each sentence. For sentences 1–5, choose the synonym of the underlined word. For sentences 6–10, choose the antonym of the underlined word.

Samples

Synonym

   A. We had a <u>wonderful</u> view of the river from our room.
- (A) sunny
- (B) everyday
- (C) spectacular
- (D) common

Antonym

   B. Mike said he felt <u>weary</u> after the long climb to the top.
- (F) lively
- (G) satisfied
- (H) proud
- (J) very tired

Choose the synonym.

1. All the students <u>congregated</u> in the gym, waiting for the exciting news.
- (A) sang
- (B) assembled
- (C) behaved
- (D) spread out

2. The police officer warned us about <u>reckless</u> bicycling in traffic.
- (F) brave
- (G) careful
- (H) damaging
- (J) irresponsible

3. Marsha said she would make a <u>contrary</u> suggestion to Mrs. O'Leary's idea.
- (A) supporting
- (B) steady
- (C) seated
- (D) opposing

4. A ship <u>glided</u> past the dock almost silently.
- (F) sped
- (G) sailed
- (H) bounced
- (J) straightened

5. Leon wrote on the board, "How can a <u>slender</u> stalk hold up such a big flower?"
- (A) green
- (B) slim
- (C) thick
- (D) wet

Choose the antonym.

6. I read a <u>humorous</u> story about a man who got stuck in a drain pipe while chasing his dog.
- (F) serious
- (G) unpleasant
- (H) laughable
- (J) warm

7. Many trained pigeons can find their way home even if they are <u>released</u> hundred of miles away.
- (A) caged
- (B) set free
- (C) taken
- (D) relocated

8. A heavy frost will <u>spoil</u> tomatoes that are still growing outside.
- (F) rot
- (G) improve
- (H) soften
- (J) stop

9. Mark was feeling <u>anxious</u> as he waited to make his speech.
- (A) relaxed
- (B) fearful
- (C) brave
- (D) feverish

10. Andrew doesn't like to play that board game. He says it's too <u>complicated</u>.
- (F) simple
- (G) involved
- (H) foolish
- (J) long

 **STOP**

Reading Comprehension: Figurative Language

Directions: Read each sentence. Look for words that have the same or almost the same meaning as the underlined phrase. Fill in the answer circle for your choice.

Samples

A. The storm <u>thundered like cannons</u> all night long above the little village.
- (A) made smoke
- (B) boomed
- (C) flashed
- (D) fired suddenly

B. He <u>roared</u>, "No!" and stomped out of the room, slamming the door behind him.
- (F) said loudly
- (G) turned into a lion
- (H) showed his teeth
- (J) shook his mane

---

1. He <u>eats like a bird</u>, no matter what kind of meal is served.
   - (A) eats in a group
   - (B) eats tiny amounts
   - (C) eats only seeds
   - (D) flutters and chirps

2. He said nothing and gave us a <u>stone-faced</u> look.
   - (F) expressionless
   - (G) rocky
   - (H) rough
   - (J) mighty

3. Sunset turned the highway into a <u>path of gold</u>.
   - (A) made it thin
   - (B) made it shine
   - (C) make it weak
   - (D) made it long

4. He <u>skipped like a lamb</u> across the open field.
   - (F) made sheep noises
   - (G) was all in white
   - (H) skipped on his hands and feet
   - (J) acted happy

5. We spent a <u>dreamy</u> afternoon watching the clouds drift past.
   - (A) sleepy
   - (B) confused
   - (C) fantasy-like
   - (D) unfriendly

6. She looked guilty and gave <u>slippery</u> answers to our questions.
   - (F) hard to hold
   - (G) wet and slick
   - (H) not quite clear
   - (J) wiggly

➤ **STOP** ◄

Reading Comprehension: Reality Versus Fantasy

Directions: In each item, read the passage and the question. Fill in the circle for your answer choice.

Sample

  A. The mayor will officially open the new public pool, located at 513 West Chapman, today at 5 P.M.

  This sentence would most likely be found in a . . .

  (A) social studies book.

  (B) newspaper article.

  (C) mystery story.

  (D) fairy tale.

---

1. The old man watched in astonishment as the elves joined hands and danced around the old tree stump, singing merrily.

    This sentence would most likely be found in a

    (A) social studies book.

    (B) newspaper article.

    (C) mystery story.

    (D) fairy tale.

---

2. "But that's impossible!" the detective insisted. "That old house has been empty for years. Who would have placed a candle in the window at midnight?"

    These sentences would most likely be found in a

    (F) social studies book.

    (G) newspaper article.

    (H) mystery story.

    (J) fairy tale.

---

3. The raft spun wildly out of control, and Evan braced himself for the waterfall ahead.

    "Evan!" Heidi shouted from the muddy bank. "I'm going to throw you a rope—catch it!"

    These sentences would most likely be found in

    (A) a social studies book.

    (B) a newspaper articie.

    (C) an adventure story.

    (D) a fairy tale.

➤ **STOP** ◄

Reading Comprehension: Main Ideas

Directions: Read the paragraphs, and fill in the correct answers.

> At one time, wolves roamed throughout North America. The most common was the timber wolf. Now, it is rare to see wolves east of the Mississippi River, but they still live in great numbers in wilder parts of the West and south to Mexico. The forests of Canada are home to wolves, too. In addition to the timber wolf, the wolves of North America include the black wolf of Florida, the red wolf of Texas, and the Arctic wolf, which is almost pure white.

1. The main idea of this paragraph is

   (A) wolves are not as dangerous as people think.

   (B) different kinds of wolves still live in North America.

   (C) wolves are becoming extinct.

   (D) wolves prefer to hunt in packs.

2. From reading this paragraph, you know it is probably true that

   (F) wolves live in the wilderness.

   (G) wolves stay away from rivers and lakes.

   (H) wolves should be left alone.

   (J) wolves are very much like dogs.

> The animal kingdom is divided into two groups. One group is the invertebrates, creatures without backbones. The second group is the vertebrates, those with backbones. All mammals, such as dogs, cats, and human beings, have backbones. A backbone is a row of small bone blocks running down a mammal's back. It is strong, and it protects the spinal cord, which is like a rope of nerves. The backbone also bends and twists, allowing its <u>owner</u> to move easily. In fact, vertebrae comes from the Latin word *vertere:* to move.

3. This paragraph explains that

   (A) the only purpose of backbones is to allow mammals to twist and turn.

   (B) humans are not mammals.

   (C) animals with backbones are stronger than those without them.

   (D) if an animal is a mammal, then it has a backbone.

GO →

4. In this paragraph, <u>owner</u> means

    (F) animal owners.

    (G) spinal cord.

    (H) mammal.

    (J) backbone.

5. What is compared in this paragraph?

    (A) the animal kingdom *to* groups

    (B) the spinal cord *to* a rope

    (C) dogs and cats *to* humans

    (D) the backbone *to* blocks of bone

> Otters are playful and affectionate animals. They have webbed feet, shiny brown fur, small ears, and long tails. They like to slide down muddy banks and snowy hills. They can be taught to fetch and to follow a person, but it is not a good idea to try to tame them. When sea otters are caught as babies and placed in zoos, they refuse to eat. Adult otters will eat if kept in a zoo, but they will not have babies.

6. If the main idea is that <u>otters are playful and affectionate</u>, then this is a supporting detail:

    (F) Adult sea otters will not have babies in zoos.

    (G) Baby sea otters will not eat in zoos.

    (H) Otters love to slide and can be taught to follow a person.

    (J) Otters have webbed feet, shiny brown fur, small ears, and long tails.

7. From reading this paragraph, you know it is probably true that

    (A) many otters live in zoos.

    (B) otters are hunted for their handsome fur.

    (C) baby otters are not placed in zoos.

    (D) otters spend most of their time playing.

➤ STOP ◄

Directions: Read the poem. Answer the questions by writing in the blank or circling the correct answer.

> Dark brown is the river,
> Golden is the sand.
> It flows along forever,
> With trees on either hand.
> Green leaves a-floating,
> Castles of the foam,
> Boats of mine a-boating—
> When will all come home?
> On goes the river,
> And out past the mill,
> Away down the valley,
> Away down the hill.
> Away down the river,
> A hundred miles or more,
> Other little children
> Shall bring my boats ashore.
>
> —Robert Louis Stevenson

1. What is the correct order that things happen in the poem?

    1—The boats float past the mill.
    2—Children find the boats.
    3—The writer puts his boats in the river.
    4—The boats float a hundred miles.

    (A) 2-1-3-4
    (B) 3-4-1-2
    (C) 3-1-4-2
    (D) 4-1-2-3

2. Write three words that could describe the boats' trip down the river.

    _____

    _____

    _____

3. Write three words that describe how the children will act when they find the boats.

    _____

    _____

    _____

4. The poet asks, "Boats of mine a-boating—/When will all come home?" Will the boats come home? Explain.

    _____

    _____

    _____

5. What is the setting of the poem?
    (A) the ocean
    (B) a forest
    (C) a river
    (D) a waterfall

6. Write a title for the poem:

    _____

    _____

➤ **STOP** ◄

Directions: Read the story, and answer the questions.

Uncle Mitya's Horse

Uncle Mitya had a very fine horse. Some thieves heard about the horse and made plans to steal it. They came after dark and climbed over the fence into Uncle Mitya's yard. Now it happened that a farmer, who had a pet bear with him, came to spend the night at Uncle Mitya's house. Uncle Mitya took the farmer into the house. Then he let the horse out of the barn into the yard. He put the bear out there, too. The thieves came into the yard and began to feel around in the dark. The bear got on his hind legs and grabbed one of the thieves, who was so frightened he screamed with all his might. Uncle Mitya and the farmer came out and caught the thieves.

—Leo Tolstoy

1. Draw a picture that shows what is described in the story.

2. The conflict in this story is
   (F) a farmer owns a dangerous bear.
   (G) thieves want to steal Uncle Mitya's horse.
   (H) where to put the bear for the night.
   (J) the thieves sneak into the yard.

3. What do you think?
   (A) Uncle Mitya wanted to catch the thieves.
   (B) The farmer brought a bear to catch the thieves.
   (C) The thieves tricked themselves into getting caught.
   (D) The thieves thought they could get along with the bear.

4. A word that could describe Uncle Mitya is
   (F) smart.
   (G) mean.
   (H) foolish.
   (J) lucky.

➤ STOP ◄

The Birds' Convention

All the birds have come together!

All the birds that I could mention,

Meet to hold a big convention!

How they cluster, how they muster,

How they flitter, flutter, fluster!

Now they dart with gleaming feather.

Now they cuddle all together!

— Aristophanes

Two Birds and Their Nest

Two guests from Alabama—two together,
And their nest, and four light-green eggs,
spotted with brown,
And every day the he-bird, to and fro, and near at hand,
And every day the she-bird, crouch'd on her nest,
silent, with bright eyes,
And every day I, a curious boy,
never too close, never disturbing them,
Cautiously peering.
— Walt Whitman

1. Which poem rhymes?
   (A) "The Birds' Convention"
   (B) "Two Birds and Their Nest"
   (C) both
   (D) none

2. Which line is meant to sound like birds?
   (F) All the birds have come together!
   (G) How they flitter, flutter, fluster!
   (H) And every day the he-bird, to and fro, and near at hand,
   (J) Two guests from Alabama—two together,

3. What is the point of view of both poems?
   (A) from someone watching the birds
   (B) from the birds' view
   (C) from below the birds
   (D) from long ago

4. The writer of the first poem sounds like he
   (F) is angered by the birds.
   (G) is entertained by them.
   (H) is wishing he could get them.
   (J) is frightened by the birds.

5. The writer of the second poem sounds like he
   (A) enjoys watching the birds.
   (B) wants them to leave.
   (C) doesn't understand what they're doing.
   (D) wants the birds to see him.

➤ **STOP** ◄

Directions: Read the passage and answer the questions.

The mice could stand it no longer. From everywhere in the house they gathered in the Great Hall of Discussion, which was really a cardboard box in the basement by the water heater.

What was the reason for their meeting? What were they upset about? They needed to decide what to do about their great enemy, the cat!

"That cat is so dangerous, she'll destroy hundreds of us!" shouted one mouse angrily.

"Thousands!" agreed another.

"Millions!" declared a third.

"Order! Order!" demanded a fat mouse with a long tail. He drummed his foot thunderously on the water heater to get everyone's attention.

"Ahem!" he began at last, when all the mice had settled down. From the corner of the basement, a cricket watched with interest.

"We are here to discuss what to do about the cat," said the fat mouse.

"She must be stopped!" squeaked a frightened voice. It came from a young mouse who had barely escaped the cat's claws—claws that were sharp as fishhooks.

"I agree," said the fat mouse. "We need protection from her. But what can we do?"

The fat mouse waited impatiently, but no one spoke.

"Well?" he asked.

In the corner, the cricket chirped.

"That's it!" cried one of the mice. He was thin and nervous looking from not daring to steal food from the kitchen for three weeks. "The cat is deadly because we can't hear her coming. We need to be able to hear her, you see?"

The mice all nodded. Yes, they understood.

"But how? What can we do to make the cat louder?" questioned the fat mouse.

"Tie a bell around her!" replied the thin mouse excitedly. "A bell on a collar around her neck. Every time she tries to sneak up on us, we'll hear the bell!"

The mice looked at each other and cheered. This was the best idea anyone had ever had for dealing with the cat. A bell! It was perfect!

They jumped up and down. The blue flame under the water heater made their shadows as big as kangaroos on the basement wall. The only mouse who wasn't acting overjoyed was an old mouse who shook his head sadly.

"All right, it's settled," said the fat mouse. "We'll tie a bell around the cat's neck, and we won't need to be afraid of her anymore. Now, who will volunteer to bell the cat?"

Silence. Most of the mice looked down, hoping not to be noticed.

Finally, the old mouse spoke up. "Yes, it's easy_____."

GO ➔

1. Finish what the old mouse said, which is the point of the story.
   (A) "Yes, it's easy to talk about the cat like this."
   (B) "Yes, it's easy to meet secretly."
   (C) "Yes, it's easy to suggest impossible ideas."
   (D) "Yes, it's easy to act excited about things."

2. What is the point of view of the story?
   (F) It's told from the mice's point of view.
   (G) It's told from the cricket's point of view.
   (H) It's told from the cat's point of view.
   (J) It's told from the writer's point of view.

3. What is the setting of the story?
   (A) the kitchen   (C) around a campfire
   (B) the basement   (D) long ago

4. Which is the best description of the plot of the story?
   (F) A cat is catching frightened mice in a house.
   (G) Mice hold a meeting to decide what to do about a cat.
   (H) An old mouse tells young mice what to do.
   (J) A cricket gives mice an idea.

5. Which is an example of figurative language in the story?
   (A) From the corner of the basement, a cricket watched with interest.
   (B) In the corner, the cricket chirped.
   (C) The blue flame under the water heater made their shadows as big as kangaroos on the basement wall.
   (D) "Every time she tries to sneak up on us, we'll hear the bell!"

6. Which is information about a mouse's character?
   (F) "Ahem!" he began at last, when all the mice had settled down.
   (G) He was thin and nervous looking from not daring to steal food from the kitchen for three weeks.
   (H) Finally, the old mouse spoke up.
   (J) It came from a young mouse who had barely escaped the cat's claws—claws that were sharp as fishhooks.

7. When the mice say the cat will destroy hundreds, thousands, millions of mice, this is an example of
   (A) plot.   (C) character.
   (B) hyperbole.   (D) point of view.

8. When "most of the mice looked down, trying not to be noticed," it's because
   (F) they are embarrassed.
   (G) they are pleased.
   (H) they are waiting for the old mouse to speak.
   (J) they are afraid.

➤ **STOP** ◄

Directions: Read the passage and answer the questions.

The ground shakes when the crust of the earth moves. This is called an earthquake. It can be caused by the crust sliding, volcanic bursts, or man-made explosions. Earthquakes that cause the most damage come from the crust sliding.

At first, the crust may only bend because of pushing forces. When the pushing becomes too much, the crust snaps and shifts into a new position. Shifting makes wiggles of energy that go out in all directions like ripples when a stone is dropped in water. These are called "seismic waves." The waves travel out from where the center of the earthquake is. Sometimes people can hear these waves. This is because they make the whole planet ring like a bell. It must be awesome to hear this sound!

The crust moving may leave a crack, or fault, in the land. Geologists, scientists who study the earth's surface, say that earthquakes often happen where there are old faults. These are weak places in the crust. Where there are faults, earthquakes may happen again and again.

When earthquakes happen under the ocean floor, they sometimes cause huge sea waves. These waves travel across the ocean as fast as 597 miles per hour and may be 49 feet high or higher. During the 1964 Alaskan earthquake, giant waves caused most of the damage to the towns of Kodiak, Cordova, and Seward. Some waves raced across the ocean in the other direction to the coasts of Japan.

Although earthquakes are usually frightening, keep in mind that the distance to the center of Earth is 3,960 miles. Most earthquakes begin less than 150 miles below the surface. Earthquakes are not a sign that the planet is unsteady.

1. Earthquakes are caused by
   (A) a giant sound under the ground.
   (B) explosions and the crust sliding.
   (C) volcanoes.
   (D) B and C
   (E) none of these.

2. Huge waves that race across the ocean can be caused by
   (F) storms.
   (G) damage.
   (H) earthquakes under the ocean.
   (J) waves as high as 49 feet.
   (K) none of these.

3. Seismic waves are compared to
   (A) ripples in water.
   (B) sounds.
   (C) a bell ringing.
   (D) faults in the ground.
   (E) none of these.

4. Which of these is an opinion?
   (F) The ground shakes when the crust of Earth moves.
   (G) It must be awesome to hear this sound!
   (H) Where there are faults, earthquakes may happen again and again.
   (J) Most earthquakes begin less than 150 miles below the surface.
   (K) none of these

GO →

5. An effect of earthquakes is
   (A) faults, or cracks, in the ground.
   (B) pushing forces building up.
   (C) 3,960 miles to the center of Earth.
   (D) a stone dropped in water.
   (E) none of these.

6. The author's purpose in this passage is
   (F) to entertain.
   (G) to persuade.
   (H) to inform.
   (J) to excuse.
   (K) none of these.

7. When earthquakes happen under the ocean floor, they sometimes cause huge sea waves. This is probably caused by
   (A) cracks in the ocean floor.
   (B) wriggles of energy.
   (C) loud noises.
   (D) weak places in the crust.
   (E) the sun being too hot.

8. Which is the correct order of events in an earthquake?
   1—The planet rings like a bell.
   2—The crust bends and snaps.
   3—Pushing forces build up under the crust.
   4—Energy is released as seismic waves.
   (F) 4-3-2-1
   (G) 1-3-2-4
   (H) 3-2-4-1
   (J) 3-4-2-1
   (K) 2-3-1-4

9. You read in the newspaper that an old fault has been discovered nearby. What may happen?
   (A) It will close up someday.
   (B) An earthquake may happen there.
   (C) People will hear seismic waves coming from it.
   (D) Earthquakes will come from much deeper there.
   (E) A flood may happen there.

10. A good title for this passage would be
    (F) Giant Waves from Nowhere.
    (G) How Earthquakes Happen.
    (H) The Mysteries of Our Earth.
    (J) Stay Put When Earthquakes Happen!
    (K) Earthquakes in Japan.

➤ **STOP** ◄

Reading Comprehension: Nonfiction 2

Directions: Read the passage below, and answer the questions.

1	To tell how old rocks are, scientists study the fossils
2	in them. Fossils give clues about what happened in
3	Earth's history. Fossils are mainly found in rock that
4	used to be mud millions of years ago. Most fossils are
5	of animals with shells and tiny parts of plants and
6	animals. Some are so small they must be studied
7	under a microscope. These are the kind scientists study
8	the most. Does the word *fossil* make you think of
9	dinosaur? Dinosaurs appear in books, movies, and
10	television programs. The bones of some large dinosaurs
11	are in many museums. These reptiles lived on Earth for
12	well over 100 million years. Many dinosaurs were quite
13	small, but some weighed as much as 80 tons! By around
14	65 million years ago, all dinosaurs were extinct. Why
15	they disappeared and what made them disappear so
16	quickly are unanswered.

1. In line #2, "them" means
   (A) rocks
   (B) scientists
   (C) fossils
   (D) dinosaurs

2. Where should a new paragraph begin?
   (F) after "most." in line #8
   (G) after "dinosaur?" in line #9
   (H) after "programs." in line # 10
   (J) after "museums." in line #11

3. In line #6, "Some" means
   (A) fossils.
   (B) animals.
   (C) shells.
   (D) parts.

4. What kind of sentence is this? "Fossils give clues about what happened in Earth's history."
   (F) a command
   (G) a question
   (H) a statement
   (J) an exclamation

5. What kind of sentence is this? "Many dinosaurs were quite small, but some weighed as much as 80 tons!"
   (A) a command
   (B) a question
   (C) a statement
   (D) an exclamation

6. Which of these sentences gives support to "Fossils give clues about what happened in the Earth's history"?
   (F) Fossils are mainly found in rock that used to be mud millions of years ago.
   (G) Most fossils are of animals with shells and tiny parts of plants and animals.
   (H) Some are so small they must be studied under a microscope.
   (J) These are the kind scientists study the most.

7. Which of the following is *not* a complete thought?
   (A) Thousands of people go to see dinosaurs in museums.
   (B) A fossil can be tiny or very large.
   (C) As much as 80 tons.
   (D) Does the word *fossil* make you think of dinosaurs?

8. A good title for this passage would be
   (F) Museums Can Be Fun and Interesting.
   (G) Fossils Are Clues to the Past.
   (H) What Happened to the Dinosaurs?
   (J) Microscopic Dinosaurs.

 **STOP**

Directions: Read the questions, and choose the best answer.

1. You are writing a report on former President Richard Milhous Nixon. Which volume of the encyclopedia would you look in?
   (A) Ru-Sap
   (B) Min-Pam
   (C) Ma-Mil
   (D) Pan-Ro

2. Now you have to look up the location and characteristics of the Sahara Desert in Northern Africa. Which volume would you choose?
   (F) Ru-Sap
   (G) Pan-Ro
   (H) Min-Pam
   (J) none of these

3. Finally, you need to look up information about the Mississippi River for social studies. Which volume would you choose?
   (A) Pan-Ro
   (B) Min-Pam
   (C) Ru-Sap
   (D) Go-Ja

4. When reading your math textbook, you are not sure of the definition of "quotient." Where would you look in your textbook for a definition?
   (F) index
   (G) table of contents
   (H) appendix
   (J) glossary

5. You need three words that have the same meaning as "slow." Where would you look?
   (A) a dictionary
   (B) a thesaurus
   (C) an encyclopedia
   (D) an atlas

GO →

6. Look at the Web site addresses below. At which one would you expect to find information about national parks?
   (F) www.campnet.com   (H) www.dep.interior.gov
   (G) www.outdoors.org   (J) www.indiana.edu

7. Which would be a topic you could research for a science fair project?
   (A) animals
   (B) Does water always boil at 212 degrees Fahrenheit?
   (C) How big is the universe?
   (D) my favorite game

For the following questions, choose A if the title sounds like fiction; B if it sounds like nonfiction.

8. *Fish in Rivers and Streams*   (A) fiction   (B) nonfiction
9. *Video Games of 1999*   (A) fiction   (B) nonfiction
10. *My Teacher Is a Martian!*   (A) fiction   (B) nonfiction
11. *Famous Women Inventors*   (A) fiction   (B) nonfiction
12. *The Ghost of the Dreadmire*   (A) fiction   (B) nonfiction

The Dewey Decimal System for Nonfiction

(A)	000–099	General Works	Encyclopedias, directories
(B)	100–199	Philosophy	Self-help, psychology
(C)	200–299	Religion	The Bible, mythology, theology
(D)	300–399	Social Science	Politics, education, folklore
(E)	400–499	Language	Languages, dictionaries
(F)	500–599	Science	Mathematics, astronomy, geology
(G)	600–699	Useful Arts	Computers, cooking, business, cars
(H)	700–799	Fine Arts	Music, painting, acting, sports
(J)	800–899	Literature	Poetry, plays, essays
(K)	900–999	History	Biography, travel, geography

Using the chart above, choose the category where you would find the following books.

13. *Favorite Mexican Tales from Folklore* by Guadalupe Ochoa
    (A)   (B)   (C)   (D)   (E)

14. *Chemistry in Medicine Today* by Dr. Alfred Noyes
    (F)   (G)   (H)   (J)   (K)

15. *The Illustrated Bible for Young People* by Morris Barker
    (A)   (B)   (C)   (D)   (E)

16. *Let's Go to Africa!* by Elwaisi Kumaguy
    (F)   (G)   (H)   (J)   (K)

17. *The Encyclopedia of Insects* by Irma Huxley
    (A)   (B)   (C)   (D)   (E)

18. *New England Recipes for Thanksgiving* by Chester L. Hooke
    (F)   (G)   (H)   (J)   (K)

➤ **STOP** ◄

Introduction

To perform your best on the mathematics section of a standardized test, you need not know the right answer every time. But you do need to use two important strategies that will improve your score: *estimating* and *recognizing a reasonable answer*.

Here's the Idea

Estimating is a way of getting close to a right answer by rounding. When you round numbers in a problem, you will get an answer that is close to the right answer.

Recognizing a reasonable answer means deciding that an answer choice is probably right, based on what you already know about numbers and problems. You can drop some answer choices right away because they are not reasonable.

However, before we look at these two skills, below are some tips that apply to taking any test, whether it is in language arts, math, science, or social studies. These tips will be repeated because they are important!

Test-Taking Tips

- **Read directions carefully before marking any test questions,** even though you have done that kind of test before. You may think you already know what the directions say, but don't ignore them—read them over. If you don't understand the directions, raise your hand and ask for help. Although your teacher must read the directions exactly as they are written, the teacher can make sure you understand what the directions mean.

- **Follow instructions.** Pay close attention to the sample exercises. They will help you understand what the items on the test will be like and how to mark your answer sheet properly.

- **Read the entire question and all the answer choices.** Do not stop reading when you have found a correct answer. Choices D or E may read "B and D" or "all of the above." On some tests, two answers are both correct. You need to read all the answer choices before marking your answer.

- **And remember—taking a test is not a race!** There are no prizes for finishing first. Use all of the time provided for the test. If you have time left over, check your answers.

Try and Discuss

Now let's discuss those two skills for mathematics tests—*estimating* and *recognizing a reasonable answer*. When you estimate, you use round numbers to come close to the correct answer without even working the problem through. Use these two rules for rounding:

- Round <u>up</u> for numbers greater than five.
- Round <u>down</u> for numbers less than five.

For example, round the numbers in this problem to find the answer—do not work the problem on paper! Just round the numbers in your mind.

		Fill in the correct circle.
23 + 16 =	(A) 7 (B) 29 (C) 39 (D) 216	Ⓐ Ⓑ Ⓒ Ⓓ

Remember the rules of rounding. Round down 23 to 20 because 3 is less than 5. Then round up 16 to 20 because 6 is greater than 5. That makes the problem in your mind 20 + 20 = (?). The answer to that problem is 40. Which answer choice is closest to 40? You can use estimating for very large problems, too. Try this one:

		Fill in the correct circle.
2,379 + 4,675	(A) 7,054 (B) 8,987 (C) 3,465 (D) 2,004	Ⓐ Ⓑ Ⓒ Ⓓ

Round down 2,379 to 2,000. Then round up 4,675 to 5,000. You can add 2,000 + 5,000 in your head. It's 7,000. Which answer comes closest? Estimating works well when you do not know the answer or you are trying to go faster on a test because time is short. Now, what about recognizing a reasonable answer? Reasonable means "likely based on careful thinking." For instance, when you see the following problem, you know that 8,000 is clearly not a reasonable answer.

		Fill in the correct circle.
20 x 4	(A) 8,000 (B) 60 (C) 80 (D) 20	Ⓐ Ⓑ Ⓒ Ⓓ

Think it through: four 20s would never total 8,000! Also, multiplying 20 by 4 could not result in 20 again—that is not a reasonable answer either. You know these things already. Recognizing a reasonable answer is a powerful strategy when you want to eliminate answers. In other words, you can drop some answer choices immediately because they are not reasonable. Don't bother with answer choices that are clearly wrong because they are unreasonable. This improves your chances of choosing the correct answer, even if you have difficulty doing the problem.

Tips That Help

Remember the following:

- Use estimating to come close to the correct answer.
- Learn to recognize a reasonable answer so you can eliminate choices that are clearly wrong.

 Now try the practice tests, listening to your teacher's directions.

Mathematics: Operations with Whole Numbers

Directions: Mark the space for the correct answer to each problem. Choose "none of these" if the right answer is not given.

Samples			
A.		**B.**	

A.

$$\begin{array}{r} 25 \\ \times\ 4 \\ \hline \end{array}$$

(A) 27
(B) 40
(C) 90
(D) 310
(E) none of these

B.

$24 \div 8 =$

(F) 4
(G) 3
(H) 6
(J) 2
(K) none of these

1.

$$\begin{array}{r} 417 \\ +\ 188 \\ \hline \end{array}$$

(A) 605
(B) 229
(C) 606
(D) 695
(E) none of these

5.

$$\begin{array}{r} 4 \\ 12 \\ 59 \\ +\ 9 \\ \hline \end{array}$$

(A) 72
(B) 82
(C) 71
(D) 62
(E) none of these

2.

$12 \div 2 =$

(F) 10
(G) 6
(H) 8
(J) 7
(K) none of these

6.

$184 + 50 + 16 =$

(F) 184
(G) 252
(H) 258
(J) 130
(K) none of these

3.

$$\begin{array}{r} 3,418 \\ 502 \\ +\ 12 \\ \hline \end{array}$$

(A) 3,930
(B) 3,932
(C) 3,922
(D) 39,220
(E) none of these

7.

$600 \div 2 =$

(A) 300
(B) 3
(C) 30
(D) 400
(E) none of these

4.

At a football game, 1,364 people sat in the grandstands. Two hundred more stood by the fence and watched. How many saw the game?

(F) 1,564
(G) 1,164
(H) 1,664
(J) 1,500
(K) none of these

8.

What is the average of 8, 12, and 16?

(F) 4
(G) 12
(H) 8
(J) 36
(K) none of these

GO →

9.

$2 \times 5 \times 4 =$

(A) 18
(B) 40
(C) 11
(D) 28
(E) none of these

10.

$$\begin{array}{r} 16 \\ \times\ 22 \\ \hline \end{array}$$

(F) 38
(G) 332
(H) 432
(J) 352
(K) none of these

11.

Four girls in two houses are each six years old. How do you show this as a multiplication problem that equals 24 years?

(A) 2 x 4
(B) 2 x 4 x 6
(C) 4 x 6
(D) 8 x 6
(E) none of these

12.

$350 \div 10 =$

(F) 3,500
(G) 35
(H) 35.1
(J) 450
(K) none of these

13.

$137 \times 20 =$

(A) 2,817
(B) 157
(C) 274
(D) 2,740
(E) none of these

14.

$67 \times 5 =$

(F) 72
(G) 335
(H) 62
(J) 330
(K) none of these

15.

There are only 101 chairs set up in the gym for the play. Three times that many are needed for the audience. How many are needed?

(A) 301
(B) 333
(C) 303
(D) 104
(E) none of these

16.

$432 \div 12 =$

(F) 40 R2
(G) 306
(H) 362
(J) 36
(K) none of these

17.

$$\begin{array}{r} 1{,}137 \\ \times\ 6 \\ \hline \end{array}$$

(A) 1,822
(B) 1,143
(C) 6,622
(D) 6,693
(E) none of these

18.

Average these numbers: 7, 3, 11.

(F) 3
(G) 7
(H) 21
(J) 13
(K) none of these

19.

$90 \div 30 =$

(A) 30
(B) 3
(C) 60
(D) 6
(E) none of these

20.

$$\begin{array}{r} 2{,}334 \\ -\ 135 \\ \hline \end{array}$$

(F) 2,199
(G) 2,469
(H) 2,201
(J) 2,109
(K) none of these

 STOP

Mathematics: Place Value and Rounding Whole Numbers

Directions: Read each item and find the correct answer. Fill in the answer circle for your choice.

Samples

A. What is another way to write a number which is 4 thousands, 8 tens, and 2 ones?

(A) 482   (C) 40,082
(B) 4,082   (D) 4,182

B. To estimate the sum of 4,215 and 6,957 to the nearest thousand, you should add

(F) 5,000 and 7,000
(G) 4,000 and 7,000
(H) 4,000 and 6,000
(J) 5,000 and 5,000

1. In which number does the 7 stand for hundreds?

(A) 7,512   (C) 3,741
(B) 5,173   (D) 6,337

2. Which number is > 5,836?

(F) 5,880   (H) 5,835
(G) 5,386   (J) 5,737

3. The newspaper said about 500 people attended a horse show. If the newspaper were rounding to the nearest ten, about how many people attended the horse show?

(A) 550
(B) 496
(C) 489
(D) 513

4. Round 21 to the nearest ten. Round 37 to the nearest ten. Multiply these two rounded numbers. The answer is

(F) 90   (H) 1,000
(G) 800   (J) 600

5. Round the numbers in the problem to the nearest ten to estimate the answer.

$$22 + 18 =$$

(A) 20   (C) 60
(B) 40   (D) 50

6. What is the value of 4 in 348,371?

(F) 400
(G) 4,000
(H) 40,000
(J) 400,000

7. Which is the largest?

(A) 4.91   (C) 4.910
(B) 49.1   (D) 4,910

8. What is the next number in this series: 30, 300, 3000, _____.

(F) 3,003   (H) 30,000
(G) 900   (J) 300,000

9. If you add a zero in the one's place to the number 393, the new number is

(A) three thousand one hundred and ninety-three.
(B) three thousand nine hundred three.
(C) three thousand ninety-three.
(D) three thousand nine hundred thirty.

10. What is this number in decimal form: eight and ninety-nine hundredths?

(F) 89.9   (H) 8.999
(G) 8.99   (J) 8.099

11. Which is the numeral for four thousand seventy-three?

(A) 4,173   (C) 40,073
(B) 4,073   (D) 4,730

12. Round the numbers in the problem to the nearest hundred to estimate the answer.

$$\begin{array}{r} 222 \\ + 888 \\ \hline \end{array}$$

(F) 1,000
(G) 1,100
(H) 1,010
(J) 1,110

> **STOP** <

Mathematics: Adding Like and Unlike Denominators

Directions: Fill in the circle for the correct answer to each addition problem. Choose "none of these" if the right answer is not given.

Samples

A.

$$\frac{2}{6}$$
$$+\ \frac{1}{6}$$

(A) 1/6
(B) 3/12
(C) 3/6
(D) 3
(E) none of these

B.

$$\frac{3}{8} + \frac{1}{4} =$$

(F) 2/4
(G) 2/8
(H) 4/12
(J) 4/8
(K) none of these

1.

$$\frac{3}{7}$$
$$+\ \frac{2}{7}$$

(A) 55/77
(B) 1/7
(C) 5/7
(D) 6/7
(E) none of these

6.

Which lists all the factors of 25?

(F) 1,5,25
(G) 1,5,20,25
(H) 1,2,5,10,20,25
(J) 2,5
(K) none of these

2.

You have two pies cut into eight pieces each. You put three pieces of one and two pieces of the other on a plate. What fraction of a pie do you have now?

(F) 1/2
(G) 5/8
(H) 6/8
(J) eighths
(K) none of these

7.

Which is not a factor of 12?

(A) 1
(B) 6
(C) 8
(D) 4
(E) none of these

3.

$$\frac{1}{8}$$
$$+\ \frac{2}{16}$$

(A) 4/8
(B) 1/8
(C) 3/8
(D) 3/16
(E) none of these

8.

What fraction of these circles is black?

(F) 2/3
(G) 3/7
(H) 7/10
(J) 3
(K) none of these

---

4. What is X if the answer is 1?

$$\frac{4}{5} + \frac{X}{10} = 1$$

(F) 5
(G) 2
(H) 1
(J) 4
(K) none of these

9.

Which is the prime factorization of 48?

(A) 2^4 x 3
(B) 2^3 x 3
(C) 2^3 x 3^2
(D) 2^5
(E) none of these

5.

Which is equal to three and three-quarters?

(A) 3 3/4
(B) 33/4
(C) 4
(D) 9/4
(E) none of these

10.

What is the least common multiple of 6 and 8?

(F) 6
(G) 14
(H) 24
(J) 8
(K) none of these

> STOP <

Mathematics: Adding Decimals

Directions: Fill in the circle for the correct answer to each addition problem. Choose "none of these" if the right answer is not given.

Samples			
A.	(A) $9.86	**B.**	(F) 8.1
	(B) $9.70		(G) 8.6
$ 5.63	(C) $9.46		(H) 7.4
+ $ 4.17	(D) $9.80	4.2 + 3.8 =	(J) 8.4
	(E) none of these		(K) none of these

1.

$ 3.48
+ $ 1.52

(A) $4.90
(B) $4.96
(C) $5.50
(D) $5.00
(E) none of these

5.
Dustin ran half of a mile in gym class in 129.6 seconds. If he ran one mile at the same speed, how many seconds would it take?

(A) 300.9
(B) 258.9
(C) 250.9
(D) 259.2
(E) none of these

2.

$ 24.18
+ $ 16.53

(F) $41.71
(G) $41.71
(H) $40.17
(J) $40.61
(K) none of these

6.
If you had $11.33 saved for a present that cost $18.80, how much more money would you need?

(F) $9.47
(G) $7.47
(H) $18.80
(J) $7.53
(K) none of these

3.

37.2 + 6.4 + 5.3 =

(A) 4.89
(B) 489
(C) 38.9
(D) 48.9
(E) none of these

7.

36.3 + 50.10 =

(A) 86.04
(B) 43.61
(C) 53.73
(D) 86.40
(E) none of these

4.

$ 22.99
+ $ 7.13

(F) $301.2
(G) $30.12
(H) $30.02
(J) $34.12
(K) none of these

8.

$ 39.99
+ $ 8.99

(F) $48.98
(G) $489.80
(H) $48.00
(J) $31.00
(K) none of these

➤ **STOP** ◄

Mathematics: Subtracting Decimals

Directions: Fill in the circle for the correct answer to each subtraction problem. Choose "none of these" if the right answer is not given.

Samples			
A. $ 67.40 − $ 14.39	(A) $53.19 (B) $53.79 (C) $53.01 (D) $81.79 (E) none of these	**B.** 0.38 − 0.21 =	(F) 1.7 (G) 1.07 (H) .59 (J) 5.9 (K) none of these

1. $ 14.01 − $ 7.17

(A) $6.84
(B) $68.40
(C) $21.18
(D) $7.04
(E) none of these

5. 8.5 − 3.9 =

(A) 4.7
(B) 12.5
(C) 12.4
(D) 5.3
(E) none of these

2. 400.0 − 0.7

(F) 40.00
(G) 399.3
(H) 399.7
(J) 370
(K) none of these

6. $ 383.00 − $ 48.53

(F) $431.53
(G) $334.53
(H) $334.47
(J) $335.47
(K) none of these

3. 6.3 − 2.8 =

(A) 623.8
(B) 9.1
(C) 3.5
(D) .35
(E) none of these

7. 12.8 − 3.8 =

(A) 9.0
(B) 15.6
(C) 90
(D) 15.0
(E) none of these

4. 9.23 − 8.47 =

(F) 76
(G) 17.70
(H) 7.6
(J) 0.76
(K) none of these

8. $ 63.41 − $ 28.05

(F) $91.46
(G) $35.36
(H) $353.60
(J) $3,536.00
(K) none of these

 **STOP**

Mathematics: Subtracting Fractions

Directions: Fill in the circle for the correct answer to each subtraction problem. Choose "none of these" if the correct answer is not given.

Samples

A.

$$\frac{5}{8} - \frac{2}{8} =$$

(A) 1

(B) 2/8

(C) 5/8

(D) 1/8

(E) none of these

B.

$$\frac{8}{11} - \frac{5}{11} =$$

(F) 13/11

(G) 4/11

(H) 3/11

(J) 3

(K) none of these

1.

$$\frac{4}{5} - \frac{1}{5} =$$

(A) 4/10

(B) 3/5

(C) 5/5

(D) 4/5

(E) none of these

5.

$$\frac{4}{7} - \frac{2}{7} =$$

(A) 6/7

(B) 6/14

(C) 8/7

(D) 2/7

(E) none of these

2.

Estimate the length of L.

M = 6

L = ?

(F) 1/2

(G) 3

(H) 8

(J) 1/6

(K) none of these

6. A square is cut into four equal pieces. One piece is taken away. What fraction of the square is left?

(F) 3

(G) 4/1

(H) 3/4

(J) 1/2

(K) none of these

3.

$$\frac{3}{6} - \frac{3}{12} =$$

(A) 6/12

(B) 9/12

(C) 0

(D) 3/12

(E) none of these

7.

Show the answer as a fraction.

(A) 2/6

(B) 2/12

(C) 6

(D) 4/6

(E) none of these

4.

$$\frac{8}{15} - \frac{7}{15} =$$

(F) 15/15

(G) 1/15

(H) 15/30

(J) 1

(K) none of these

8.

$$\frac{1}{3} - \frac{2}{9} =$$

(F) 3/9

(G) 1/9

(H) 2/3

(J) 3/27

(K) none of these

➤ **STOP** ◄

Mathematics: Mixed Numbers

Directions: Fill in the circle for the correct answer to each problem. Choose "none of these" if the right answer is not given.

Samples

A.

$$4 \frac{1}{4}$$
$$- 2 \frac{1}{4}$$
_____

   (A) 2 1/4
   (B) 2 2/4
   (C) 6 2/4
   (D) 2
   (E) none of these

B.

$$5 \frac{2}{8}$$
$$+ 3 \frac{1}{8}$$
_____

   (F) 8 2/8
   (G) 8 1/8
   (H) 2 1/8
   (J) 8 3/8
   (K) none of these

1.

$$4$$
$$- 1 \frac{1}{3}$$
_____

   (A) 3
   (B) 3 2/3
   (C) 2 2/3
   (D) 5 1/3
   (E) none of these

5.

A box of butter has four quarter-pound sticks of butter in it. How much does a box of butter weigh?

   (A) four pounds
   (B) one pound
   (C) one-half pound
   (D) one-quarter pound
   (E) none of these

2.

$$5 \frac{1}{13}$$
$$+ 4 \frac{11}{13}$$
_____

   (F) 9 10/13
   (G) 1 10/13
   (H) 9 12/13
   (J) 1 0/13
   (K) none of these

6.

 =

   (F) 2 1/2
   (G) 1 1/2
   (H) 4 1/2
   (J) 3 1/2
   (K) none of these

3.

It takes 2 1/2 minutes to make a chocolate milkshake. Three children order milkshakes. How long will it take to make them?

   (A) 10 minutes
   (B) 12 1/2 minutes
   (C) 7 1/2 minutes
   (D) 25 1/2 minutes
   (E) none of these

7.

$$5 \ 4/9 + 5 \ 2/9 =$$

   (A) 7 11/10
   (B) 10 1/3
   (C) 6/9
   (D) 10 8/9
   (E) none of these

4.

$$8 \ 5/8 - 6 \ 5/8 =$$

   (F) 2 10/8
   (G) 2 3/8
   (H) 2 5/8
   (J) 2
   (K) none of these

8.

$$9$$
$$- 3 \frac{3}{4}$$
_____

   (F) 4 1/4
   (G) 5 1/4
   (H) 6 3/4
   (J) 6 1/4
   (K) none of these

➤ **STOP** ◄

Mathematics: Problem Solving

Directions: Read the story problems, and answer the questions. Fill in the choice for "none of these" if no answer is correct.

Mrs. Ramirez, a fourth-grade teacher, will show a video for 30 minutes. If it is longer than that, she will continue it the next day.

Video Running Times	
Rip Van Winkle	90 minutes
Jumpin' Sam Patch	20 minutes
Pueblo Days	30 minutes
How Chicks Hatch	40 minutes

1. How many days will it take Mrs. Ramirez to show *Rip Van Winkle*?
   - (A) 2.7 days
   - (B) 3 days
   - (C) 2 days
   - (D) 120 minutes
   - (E) none of these

2. Which video could she show in less than one day?
   - (F) *How Chicks Hatch*
   - (G) *Pueblo Days*
   - (H) *Rip Van Winkle*
   - (J) *Jumpin' Sam Patch*
   - (K) none of these

3. Which two videos would come out to two 30-minute showings exactly?
   - (A) *How Chicks Hatch* and *Pueblo Days*
   - (B) *Jumpin' Sam Patch* and *How Chicks Hatch*
   - (C) *Jumpin' Sam Patch* and *Pueblo Days*
   - (D) *Rip Van Winkle*
   - (E) none of these

4. In a dart-throwing game, Darnell threw eight times and hit the target every fourth time. How many times did he hit the target?
   - (F) 6
   - (G) 8
   - (H) 2
   - (J) 12
   - (K) none of these

5. André has set a reading goal. He's going to read two books every week for a month. How many books will he read in two months?
   - (A) 16
   - (B) 4
   - (C) 64
   - (D) 30
   - (E) none of these

GO →

6. Tran has five adventure game CDs in his collection. His cousin is one year older than he is and has twice as many. How would you show the problem for how many CDs Tran's cousin has?

    (F) 5 x 2 + 1

    (G) 6 x 2

    (H) 1 + 3 + 5

    (J) 5 + 1 x 2

    (K) none of these

7. Berneitha, Karen, and Tamika went trick or treating on Halloween. Berneitha got seven pieces of gum; Karen got three; and Tamika got two. What was the average number of pieces of gum each girl received?

    (A) 3

    (B) 4

    (C) 6

    (D) 12

    (E) none of these

8. For the food drive at school, 16 students are each bringing 7 cans. How many cans will they bring?

    (F) 23

    (G) 112

    (H) 122

    (J) 118

    (K) none of these

9. There are 30 children in gym class. Every fifth child is going to be a team leader. If the first team leader is child number 5 and the second team leader is child number 10, what number will the fourth team leader be?

    (A) 15

    (B) 25

    (C) 20

    (D) 30

    (E) none of these

10. Angela bought a candy bar at the movie theater. She gave the boy at the counter four quarters. He gave her two dimes in change. How much did the candy bar cost?

    (F) $.75

    (G) $.80

    (H) $1.20

    (J) $.90

    (K) none of these

➤ **STOP** ◄

Mathematics: Customary and Metric Units

Directions: Read the questions and circle the correct answer.

1. What is the Roman numeral for 29?
   - (A) XXXI
   - (B) XXXVIV
   - (C) XXVIIII
   - (D) XVVIIII

2. In four months, Margaret's brother Tim will be one year old. How old is Tim now?
   - (F) five months
   - (G) seven months
   - (H) six months
   - (J) eight months

3. Ron wants to make a special kind of punch that needs 1/2 gallon of ginger ale. He has a quart of ginger ale in the refrigerator. How much more does he need?
   - (A) 3 quarts
   - (B) 2 quarts
   - (C) 1 quart
   - (D) 2 cups

4. A package of cookies says there are two dozen inside. How many are in there?
   - (F) 20
   - (G) 22
   - (H) 12
   - (J) 24

Trains to University Park

Name	Leaves	Arrives
Flyer	5:02 P.M.	5:40 P.M.
Red Line	5:30 P.M.	6:10 P.M.
Sunset	5:45 P.M. *(makes one stop)*	6:30 P.M.

---

5. How long does the Flyer take to get to University Park?
   - (A) 38 minutes
   - (B) 1 hour, 2 minutes
   - (C) 42 minutes
   - (D) 36 minutes

6. How long does the Red Line take to get to University Park?
   - (F) 40 minutes
   - (G) 20 minutes
   - (H) 50 minutes
   - (J) 1 hour, 10 minutes

GO ➡

7. If the Sunset goes as fast as the Red Line train, how much time does the extra stop take?

   (A) 5 minutes

   (B) 10 minutes

   (C) 1 hour, 15 minutes

   (D) 15 minutes

8. What is the total value of these coins?

   (F) $.44

   (G) $.36

   (H) $.54

   (J) $.64

9. If July 4th is on a Wednesday, what day of the week will July 11th be?

   (A) Tuesday

   (B) Wednesday

   (C) Monday

   (D) Thursday

10. About how tall is a regular door?

    (F) 72 inches

    (G) 7 feet

    (H) 12 feet

    (J) 12 inches

11. Two meters is how many centimeters?

    (A) 20

    (B) 200

    (C) 2,000

    (D) 20,000

12. A kilogram is 1,000 grams. Marc picked 3 kilograms of blueberries at a farm in Michigan. His mom used 2,000 grams for muffins. How many kilograms of blueberries are left over?

    (F) 2

    (G) 1/2

    (H) 1

    (J) 5

GO →

13. Grandpa Morgan's deck behind his house is 18 feet wide. How many yards wide is it?

    (A) 6

    (B) 3

    (C) 15

    (D) 9

14. How long is this pencil?

    (F) 2 1/2 inches

    (G) 2 1/4 inches

    (H) 2 3/4 inches

    (J) .23 inches

    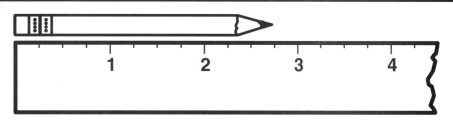

15. A quart of milk is half empty. How many cups are left?

    (A) 2

    (B) 4

    (C) 6

    (D) 1

16. A spaghetti recipe calls for one pound of stewed tomatoes. Robby has a can of stewed tomatoes in the cupboard that is "32 oz." How many pounds is the can in the cupboard?

    (F) 4

    (G) 2

    (H) 1

    (J) 3

17. How many degrees difference are there between thermometer A and B?

    (A) 24 degrees

    (B) 26 degrees

    (C) 8 degrees

    (D) 40 degrees

    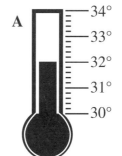
    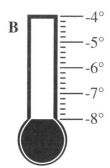

18. There are 2.54 centimeters in an inch. About how many centimeters are there in 1 foot?

    (F) 10

    (G) 20

    (H) 30

    (J) 60

➤ STOP ◄

Mathematics: Geometry

Directions: Read each question and find the correct answer. Fill in the answer circle for your choice.

Samples

A. These are the dimensions of Mr. Dominic's garden. What is the area of his garden?

50 feet

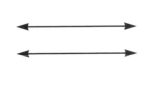

15 feet

   (A) 65 square feet

   (B) 45 square feet

   (C) 750 square feet

   (D) 550 square feet

B. Which pair of lines is parallel?

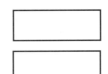
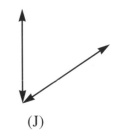

    (F)   (G)   (H)   (J)

---

1. Which answer shows a pair of congruent figures?

    (A)   (B)   (C)   (D)

---

2. What is the perimeter of this polygon if all sides are equal?

    (F) 36 feet   (H) 24 feet

    (G) 32 feet   (J) 16 feet

4 feet

---

3. What is the diameter of the circle?

    (A) 36 in.   (C) 12 in.

    (B) 18.35 in.   (D) 24 in.

6 in.

---

4. Which of these is a cone?

    (F)   (G)   (H)   (J)

GO ➡

5. Name two lines that intersect.

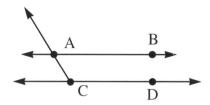

(A) $\overline{AC}, \overline{BD}$
(B) $\overline{AB}, \overline{CD}$
(C) $\overline{AC}, \overline{AB}$
(D) $\overline{CA}, \overline{AC}$

6. Which of these is a right angle?

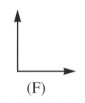  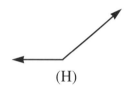

(F)   (G)   (H)   (J)

7. In this figure, which is the vertex?

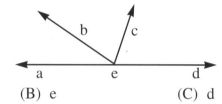

(A) b   (B) e   (C) d   (D) c

8. Which of these has planes you can't see?

(F)   (G)   (H)   (J)

9. Which has more volume?

(A) a one-gallon jug

(B) a plastic bowl that can hold eight cups

(C) a quart bottle

(D) a balloon that can hold two pints

10. What number is the arrow pointing to?

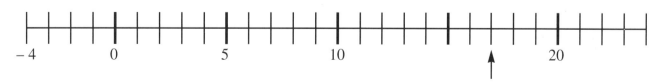

(F) 12   (G) -26   (H) 17   (J) 13

➤ **STOP** ◄

Introduction

Science tries to uncover the physical truth about the way things work—how the seasons change, why animals hibernate, or what kinds of rock are created by volcanoes, for example. To perform your best on questions about science, you must pay attention to important words in each question that might make the answer choices true or untrue.

Here's the Idea

People who work in science try to find out what is true and what is untrue. Questions on science tests often have words in them, such as *not, but, except, always, never,* and *only,* which make answer choices true or untrue. You must watch for these key words in the test questions.

However, before we look at these key words, below are some tips that apply to taking any test, whether it is in language arts, math, science, or social studies. These tips will be repeated because they are important!

Test-Taking Tips

- **Read directions carefully before marking any test questions**, even though you have done that kind of test before. You may think you already know what the directions say, but don't ignore them—read them over. If you don't understand the directions, raise your hand and ask for help. Although your teacher must read the directions exactly as they are written, the teacher can make sure you understand what the directions mean.

- **Follow instructions.** Pay close attention to the sample exercises. They will help you understand what the items on the test will be like and how to mark your answer sheet properly.

- **Read the entire question and all the answer choices.** Do not stop reading when you have found a correct answer. Choices D or E may read "B and D" or "all of the above." On some tests, two answers are both correct. You need to read all the answer choices before marking your answer.

- **For long reading passages, read the questions first so you know what to look for.** If you read the questions first, you'll find information in the passage that answers the questions.

- **Remember that taking a test is not a race!** There are no prizes for finishing first. Use all of the time provided for the test. If you have time left over, check your answers.

Try and Discuss

Let's discuss those key words in many science questions: *not, but, except, always, never*, and *only*. Words such as *not, but, except, always, never,* and *only* make a big difference—but you must be alert for these words. Look at these questions.

Which of the following is not part of the circulatory system?

(A) heart

(B) bones   Fill in the correct circle.

(C) blood vessels   Ⓐ   Ⓑ   Ⓒ   Ⓓ

(D) blood

At first glance, "blood" might seem like the odd one here because it is a liquid—it's not a solid object like the others. But read the question carefully: "Which of the following is *not* part of the circulatory system?" It's not asking "Which one does not belong?" The circulatory system does not include bones so (B) "bones" is the correct answer.

Now look at the following question:

A cabbage has stems and leaves. Which is the only one with scales and bones?

(A) frog
(B) cat   Fill in the correct circle.

(C) fish   Ⓐ   Ⓑ   Ⓒ   Ⓓ

(D) human

Now, all of these choices have bones, so you may be confused for a moment. But look carefully: the questions asks, "Which is the *only* one with scales and bones?" Only one has both: (C) "fish."

Tips That Help

Remember the following:

- People who work in science try to find out what is true and untrue.

- Pay attention to key words in science questions, such as *not, but, except, always, never,* and *only,* that will make answer choices true or untrue.

 Now try the practice tests, listening to your teacher's directions.

Directions: Read the questions, and choose the best answer. In some places, you are asked to write your answers.

1. Let's compare and contrast two plants. List information that you know or can see about each plant.

Plant 1	**Plant 2**
• _____	• _____
• _____	• _____
• _____	• _____
• _____	• _____
• _____	• _____

2. All living things need
   (F) seeds.
   (G) energy.
   (H) soil.
   (J) leaves.

3. Seeds develop in a part of a plant called a
   (A) root.
   (B) stem.
   (C) leaf.
   (D) flower.

4. All plants and animals have this in common:
   (F) straightness.
   (G) photosynthesis.
   (H) respiration.
   (J) usefulness.

5. A rose has stems and leaves. Which of the following has scales and bones?
   (A) frog
   (B) cat
   (C) fish
   (D) human

6. Any matter that can be made into useful products is called
   (F) stored food.
   (G) raw material.
   (H) light.
   (J) energy.

GO →

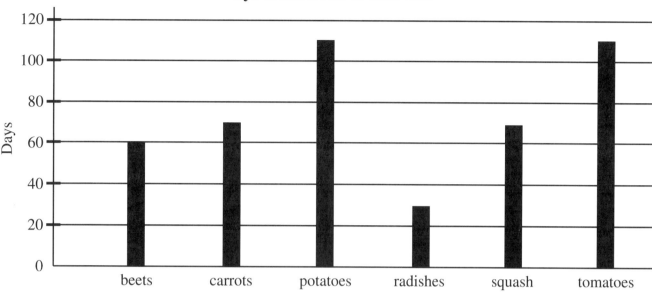

Days from Seed to Harvest

Kyle is planning a vegetable garden. He uses this bar graph above to help him.

7. How long does it take carrots to grow?
   (A) 60 days
   (B) 70 days
   (C) 65 days
   (D) 61 days

8. Which vegetable will be ready the soonest?
   (F) beets
   (G) carrots and squash
   (H) radishes
   (J) potatoes and tomatoes

9. Which vegetables should he plant first to make sure they have enough time to grow?
   (A) radishes
   (B) beets
   (C) carrots and squash
   (D) potatoes and tomatoes

10. Which vegetable could he plant and harvest about three times before the last vegetables were ready?
    (F) radishes
    (G) beets
    (H) squash
    (J) potatoes and tomatoes

> **STOP** <

Directions: Read the questions, and choose the best answer.

1. One of the most important activities for animals is
   (A) flying.
   (B) being warm.
   (C) finding food.
   (D) being together.

2. Anything an animal does is its
   (F) mind.
   (G) behavior.
   (H) coloring.
   (J) name.

3. Behavior an animal is born with is
   (A) learned behavior.
   (B) easily changed.
   (C) social behavior.
   (D) inborn behavior.

4. Behavior that is learned can be
   (F) changed.
   (G) imprinted.
   (H) a reflex.
   (J) instinct.

5. Which is not an example of animal instinct?
   (A) playing with a ball
   (B) hunting for food
   (C) spinning a web
   (D) migrating

6. Any area an animal defends against its enemies is its
   (F) territory.
   (G) home.
   (H) right.
   (J) nest.

7. A bird's wings or a duck's webbed feet are examples of
   (A) coloring.
   (B) behavior.
   (C) adaptation.
   (D) skill.

8. If a scientist wanted to study animal behavior, why would a zoo not be a good place to do it?
   (F) The animals wouldn't like being watched.
   (G) It would take too long.
   (H) Animal behavior is different in zoos than in the wild.
   (J) There aren't enough animals to study in zoos.

9. Which of these does not belong?
   (A) camouflage
   (B) mouth parts
   (C) protection
   (D) changing colors

10. They belong to packs. They defend themselves against newcomers. They have a leader. This describes
    (F) ants.
    (G) wolves.
    (H) fish.
    (J) prairie dogs.

➤ **STOP** ◄

Directions: Read the questions, and choose the best answer.

1. Thick layers of rotted trees and plants in tropical swamps form

   (A) granite.

   (B) marble.

   (C) limestone.

   (D) coal.

2. In a forest, you find a tiny fossil of a fish. How can this be?

   (F) The fossil was carried there by the wind.

   (G) The fish was dropped on the forest floor many years ago.

   (H) The forest was once under water.

   (J) The forest is making new fossils.

3. Which does not belong in this group?

   (A) iron

   (B) quartz

   (C) copper

   (D) aluminum

4. What is the correct order of the water cycle?

   1—The sun heats ocean water.

   2—Water evaporates from the ocean.

   3—Water returns to Earth as rain.

   4—Clouds form from evaporated water.

   (F) 3-2-1-4

   (G) 1-2-4-3

   (H) 3-1-4-2

   (J) 2-3-1-4

5. How much does this rock weigh?

   (A) 3 lbs.

   (B) 3 1/2 lbs.

   (C) 4 lbs.

   (D) 5 lbs.

   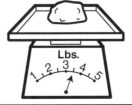

6. A scientist who studies Earth is a

   (F) biologist.

   (G) geologist.

   (H) archeologist.

   (J) nutritionist.

7. The ocean floor is like the surface of dry land in this way:

   (A) many of the same animals live on both.

   (B) there are mountains, volcanoes, and valleys.

   (C) they have the same seasons.

   (D) both can be warm or cold.

8. What is the correct order?

   1—Pressure and cementing change sediments to sedimentary rock.

   2—The buildup of layers becomes heavy.

   3—Sediment collects in layers at the bottoms of oceans, rivers, and lakes.

   4—Minerals dissolved in water cement the sediments together.

   (F) 4-3-1-2

   (G) 2-3-1-4

   (H) 3-1-2-4

   (J) 3-2-4-1

➤ **STOP** ◄

Science: The Solar System

Directions: Read the questions, and choose the best answer.

1. Which words belong together?

    (A) star, sun, crater, water

    (B) comet, tail, ice, light

    (C) star, comet, blast, rings

    (D) Mars, sunspots, rocket, ice

2. Sun is to star as Earth is to

    (F) moon.

    (G) orbit.

    (H) planet.

    (J) bright.

3. Which picture shows the correct position of Earth, the sun, and the moon during a solar eclipse?

Key
Earth (O)
sun (**O**)
moon (o)

    (A) o   O   o

    (B) O   o   o

    (C) o   o   O

    (D) O   o   O

4. The center of the solar system is

    (F) Earth.

    (G) the sun.

    (H) the Milky Way.

    (J) the universe.

5. How long is a day on Earth?

    (A) 12 hours

    (B) 24 hours

    (C) 10 hours

    (D) 8 hours

6. When Earth receives the most direct sunlight, it is

    (F) winter.

    (G) spring.

    (H) summer.

    (J) fall.

7. In our solar system, the planet with rings is

    (A) Pluto.

    (B) Mars.

    (C) the sun.

    (D) Saturn.

8. Meteorites striking the surface of the moon cause

    (F) volcanoes.

    (G) craters.

    (H) dust storms.

    (J) magnetism.

9. The greatest number of sunspots have appeared on the sun in these years:

    1946   1957   1968   1979   1990

    If the pattern continues, predict when the greatest number of sunspots will appear again.

    (A) 1999

    (B) 2001

    (C) 2068

    (D) 1998

10. The planets stay in orbit because of

    (F) size.

    (G) speed.

    (H) atmosphere.

    (J) gravity.

➤ **STOP** ◄

Science: Electricity and Magnetism

Directions: Read the questions, and choose the best answer.

1. The smallest part of matter is

   (A) an atom.

   (B) an electron.

   (C) a proton.

   (D) a neutron.

2. Which is not a true statement?

   (F) Objects with opposite charges attract.

   (G) A magnet is an object that will attract some materials.

   (H) All atoms attract each other.

   (J) Objects with the same charge repel, or push away from, each other.

3. When clothes cling together in the dryer, or make a crackling sound, this is an example of

   (A) charging up.

   (B) proton newness.

   (C) static electricity.

   (D) light being made.

4. Which is an example of a hypothesis?

   (F) The experiment will take one hour.

   (G) The experiment will show that plastic is not magnetic.

   (H) The experiment is about electricity.

   (J) The experiment needs two partners wearing gloves.

5. For a science fair project, you are going to prove which kind of battery lasts the longest—a Glow-on or an Everlight. Which experiment would be the best to prove this?

   (A) Put the fresh batteries into two different kinds of toys. Turn the toys on. Record which one stops first.

   (B) Take a Glow-on battery and an Everlight battery from electronic games and test how strong they are.

   (C) Take two of the same kind of flashlight. Put fresh Glow-on batteries in one and fresh Everlight batteries in the other. Turn both on. Record which one goes out first.

   (D) Ask people which kind of battery they like and why.

GO →

6. Which makes a good insulator?

    (F) metal wire

    (G) rubber

    (H) water

    (J) glass

7. Magnetic force on Earth is strongest

    (A) in the oceans.

    (B) at the north and south poles.

    (C) near volcanoes.

    (D) opposite the moon.

8. The center of an atom is called

    (F) the proton.

    (G) the nucleus.

    (H) the electron.

    (J) the neutron.

9. The movement of electrons along a path is called

    (A) a current.

    (B) a circuit.

    (C) a field.

    (D) a site.

10. You can feel the effect of a magnetic field with

    (F) a compass.

    (G) a generator.

    (H) two magnets.

    (J) a power plant.

➤ **STOP** ◄

Science: Health and Nutrition

Directions: Read the questions, and choose the best answer.

1. The heart, blood vessels, and blood make up parts of the

   (A) digestive system.

   (B) circulatory system.

   (C) nervous system.

   (D) skeletal system.

2. Which is not an organ?

   (F) liver

   (G) brain

   (H) hand

   (J) stomach

3. An activity that uses the muscles of the body can be called

   (A) digestion.

   (B) exercise.

   (C) breathing.

   (D) pulse.

4. Margaret has a cold. The most important thing she should do to keep from spreading the cold to others is

   (F) get plenty of rest.

   (G) wash her hands frequently.

   (H) try not to sneeze.

   (J) take her temperature regularly.

5. Which of these food groups provide vitamin C?

   (A) meat

   (B) milk

   (C) grain

   (D) fruits and vegetables

6. Angie says she wants to make sure she has enough energy to play baseball for long hours. She should make sure she is eating enough

   (F) carbohydrates.

   (G) fat.

   (H) proteins.

   (J) minerals.

7. Strong bones and teeth need

   (A) protein.

   (B) calcium.

   (C) growth.

   (D) pasta.

8. A liquid nutrient your body needs most is

   (F) blood.

   (G) iron.

   (H) milk.

   (J) water.

9. What could you add to a lunch of milk, eggs, and an orange so that it includes all food groups?

   (A) bread

   (B) chicken

   (C) apple juice

   (D) cheese

10. Which food would be the highest in calories?

    (F) a tomato

    (G) an apple

    (H) a pretzel

    (J) butter

 ➤ **STOP** ◄

Introduction

Social studies is all about people and places. It can be difficult at times to remember many names and events. But to perform your best on a social studies section, it helps to ask yourself a question about the question!

Here's the Idea

A social studies question may be about a region, a president, or an event. It helps focus your attention on what the question is asking—and it helps you eliminate choices, too—if you ask yourself *who, what, where, when,* or *how*?

However, before we look at these key words, below are some tips that apply to taking any test, whether it is in language arts, math, science, or social studies. These tips are repeated because they are important!

Test-Taking Tips

- **Read directions carefully before marking any test questions**, even though you have done that kind of test before. You may think you already know what the directions say, but don't ignore them—read them over. If you don't understand the directions, raise your hand and ask for help. Although your teacher must read the directions exactly as they are written, the teacher can make sure you understand what the directions mean.

- **Follow instructions.** Pay close attention to the sample exercises. They will help you understand what the items on the test will be like and how to mark your answer sheet properly.

- **Read the entire question and all the answer choices.** Do not stop reading when you have found a correct answer. Choices D or E may read "B and D" or "all of the above." On some tests, two answers are both correct. You need to read all the answer choices before marking your answer.

- **For long reading passages, read the questions first so you know what to look for.** If you read the questions first, you'll find information in the passage that answers the questions.

- **Remember that taking a test is not a race!** There are no prizes for finishing first. Use all of the time provided for the test. If you have time left over, check your answers.

Try and Discuss

Let's discuss asking the questions: *who, what, where, when,* or *how.* Social studies questions are about persons, places, or events and when or how they happened.

For example, here is a social studies test question:

A major industry of the Midwest region is

Fill in the correct circle.

(A) agriculture.
(B) Illinois, Ohio, Wisconsin, Iowa, and Michigan.
(C) fishing.
(D) the Civil War.

Ask yourself, "Is this a question about *who, what, where, when,* or *how?*" It asks about "a major industry." It is asking *what,* <u>not</u> *where,* which eliminates choice (B) right away. The correct answer is (A) agriculture.

Look at the list of topics below. Would they probably be asking *who, what, where, when,* or *how?* (You may be right sometimes if you suggest more than one.)

- maps

- climate

- resources

- people

- history

Tips That Help

Social studies is all about people and places. It can be difficult at times to remember lots of names and events. But to perform your best on a social studies section, it helps to ask yourself a question about the question: *who, what, where, when,* or *how.*

Now try the practice tests, listening to your teacher's directions.

Social Studies: Maps and Globes

Directions: Read the questions, and choose the best answer.

Samples

A. Which of the following is an example of a resource?
(A) forests
(B) skyscrapers
(C) corn
(D) climate

B. Which is the smallest continent?
(F) North America
(G) Australia
(H) Africa
(J) Asia

1. How would you best describe a continent?
   (A) mountains, valleys, and streams
   (B) a globe
   (C) a large land mass
   (D) a point on a map

2. Which pair does not belong?
   (F) latitude, longitude
   (G) high, low
   (H) degrees, minutes
   (J) Eastern Hemisphere, Western Hemisphere

3. Which of the following are not landforms?
   (A) mountains and valleys
   (B) hills and plains
   (C) boundaries and state lines
   (D) islands and rivers

4. You could use a map or globe for each of the following except
   (F) finding your location on the planet.
   (G) finding out about the culture of a country.
   (H) finding which continent is the smallest.
   (J) finding the countries in Europe.

5. A _____ is a powerful flow of water in the ocean.
   (A) stream
   (B) current
   (C) wave
   (D) shoreline

6. Which of the following is not a continent?
   (F) Europe
   (G) South America
   (H) Australia
   (J) Mexico

7. The Northern and the Southern Hemispheres are divided by
   (A) the prime meridian.
   (B) water.
   (C) longitude.
   (D) the equator.

8. Where is Puerto Rico located?
   (F) in the Indian Ocean
   (G) in the Caribbean Sea
   (H) in the Atlantic Ocean
   (J) in Mexico

9. The United States is located _____ of Central America.
   (A) south
   (B) north
   (C) west
   (D) east

10. The United States is bounded by these bodies of water except
    (F) the Pacific Ocean.
    (G) the Atlantic Ocean.
    (H) the Gulf of Mexico.
    (J) the Indian Ocean.

➤ STOP ◄

Social Studies: United States Regions and History 1

Directions: Read the questions, and choose the best answer. More than one answer may be correct.

Samples

A. As settlers moved into the Middle Atlantic region, what did they discover about the land?

   (A) It was dry and harsh.

   (B) It was more mountainous.

   (C) It offered many crops growing wild.

   (D) It was not easy to farm.

B. Which city did not become a location for trade?

   (F) Philadelphia

   (G) Boston

   (H) New York

   (J) Washington, D.C.

---

1. Which of the following is a true statement?

   (A) A region is an area that shares a mountain range.

   (B) Each state in the United States is a region.

   (C) A region is an area of land that has one or more characteristics in common.

   (D) The Mississippi River divides the United States into two regions, East and West.

2. On a climate map, you would expect to see

   (F) animals.

   (G) temperature.

   (H) favorite vacation spots.

   (J) average depth of bodies of water.

3. You will find prairies located in

   (A) the Midwest and Great Plains.

   (B) New England.

   (C) the Southwest.

   (D) the Pacific West.

4. Which is not a true statement?

   (F) The southwestern part of the United States is drier.

   (G) Higher mountains are located in the western part of the United States.

   (H) The Great Plains are located west of the Rocky Mountains.

   (J) There are deserts in the western part of the United States.

5. The Mississippi River does not touch which of these states?

   (A) Illinois

   (B) Texas

   (C) Missouri

   (D) Louisiana

6. Which is not a natural boundary?

   (F) a mountain range

   (G) a highway

   (H) a coastline

   (J) a river

GO →

7. Why are the boundaries of Eastern states, such as Virginia and Ohio, not rectangular like Western states?

   (A) The study of geography had not begun.

   (B) No one could chart a straight line for hundreds of miles.

   (C) The eastern states used natural boundaries for state lines.

   (D) The land is rougher in the East than the West.

8. The original thirteen states had been _____ of Great Britain.

   (F) territories

   (G) regions

   (H) kingdoms

   (J) colonies

9. The number of people in a region is its _____.

   (A) population

   (B) census

   (C) democracy

   (D) mass

10. Which one of the following is not a New England state?

    (F) Maine

    (G) New Hampshire

    (H) Ohio

    (J) Massachusetts

11. Why did the first groups of English settlers come to the New World?

    (A) to look for gold

    (B) to spread their religion around the world

    (C) to find a new route to the East Indies

    (D) to practice their religion openly

12. The most important cause of the American Revolution was

    (F) the price of goods in Boston was too high.

    (G) England was too far away to communicate with.

    (H) whaling was too difficult at which to make a living.

    (J) Americans were not represented in England's government.

13. The United States shares its longest border with

    (A) New England.

    (B) Canada.

    (C) Mexico.

    (D) Central America.

14. Which is an example of a raw material?

    (F) roads

    (G) coal

    (H) cement

    (J) televisions

15. Where was the Declaration of Independence signed?

    (A) New York City, New York

    (B) Washington, D.C.

    (C) Boston, Massachusetts

    (D) Philadelphia, Pennsylvania

16. The Grand Canyon was formed by

    (F) wind and rain.

    (G) the Colorado River.

    (H) volcanoes.

    (J) earthquakes.

➤ **STOP** ◄

Directions: Read the questions, and choose the best answer. More than one answer may be correct.

Samples

A. Which city is known as the Mile High City?

(A) Los Angeles

(B) Chicago

(C) Denver

(D) Salt Lake City

B. Which industry is not found in Texas?

(F) ranching

(G) oil refining

(H) pineapple growing

(J) dairy farming

---

1. The purpose of building canals was to

   (A) move people faster than the railroad could.

   (B) speed the movement of people and products.

   (C) irrigate farmlands.

   (D) spread fishing throughout the states.

2. Which of the following is an example of an import?

   (F) a car made in Germany and shipped to New York

   (G) corn sent from Illinois to Russia

   (H) glass sent from Pittsburgh to Detroit

   (J) computers made in California and sold in stores

3. Why is Washington, D.C., in the District of Columbia rather than a state?

   (A) The district is land that is not part of any state.

   (B) The district is in the middle of the nation.

   (C) The district is near the Atlantic Ocean for travel.

   (D) The district is just the right size for the national capital.

4. Which event led to the start of the Civil War?

   (F) Escaped slaves revolted in the South.

   (G) Abraham Lincoln was elected president.

   (H) The southern states formed a Confederacy.

   (J) Southern troops fired on Fort Sumter.

5. Which crop was called "king" in the South and grown on large estates?

   (A) tomatoes

   (B) cotton

   (C) potatoes

   (D) corn

6. Why did New Orleans become a major center of trade?

   (F) It is located near major water routes.

   (G) It is located in the Deep South.

   (H) It was not involved in the Civil War.

   (J) It was once part of the French empire.

GO →

Social Studies: United States Regions and History 2 *(cont.)*

7. All of the following are located in the Midwest except

   (A) the Mississippi River.

   (B) Lake Michigan.

   (C) the Rio Grande.

   (D) the Missouri River.

8. Which is not a chief product of the Midwest?

   (F) steel

   (G) wheat

   (H) cotton

   (J) lumber

9. Which of these is a service job?

   (A) farmer

   (B) astronaut

   (C) restaurant worker

   (D) auto factory worker

10. All of the following are associated with the Southwest except

    (F) oil.

    (G) gold.

    (H) cattle.

    (J) barley.

11. Which is not a southwestern state?

    (A) Texas

    (B) Oregon

    (C) Arizona

    (D) New Mexico

12. Which natural resource is in short supply in the Southwest?

    (F) water

    (G) minerals

    (H) natural gas

    (J) ore

13. What was a major reason people went to California in the mid-1800s?

    (A) freedom

    (B) the discovery of gold

    (C) the discovery of oil

    (D) whaling

14. What means of transportation made travel to the West much faster after the Civil War?

    (F) steamships

    (G) railroads

    (H) airplanes

    (J) sailing ships

15. Native Americans, surrounded by settlers coming west, were moved by the United States government to

    (A) plantations.

    (B) national parks.

    (C) canyons.

    (D) reservations.

16. The most recent territories to have become states are

    (F) Puerto Rico and Guam.

    (G) the United States Virgin Islands and Jamaica.

    (H) Hawaii and Alaska.

    (J) the Philippines and Marshall Islands.

➤ **STOP** ◄

Student Answer Sheets

Writing: Syllabication
Test page: 19

Samples
- A. Ⓐ Ⓑ Ⓒ
- B. Ⓕ Ⓖ Ⓗ

Test
1. Ⓐ Ⓑ Ⓒ
2. Ⓕ Ⓖ Ⓗ
3. Ⓐ Ⓑ Ⓒ
4. Ⓕ Ⓖ Ⓗ
5. Ⓐ Ⓑ Ⓒ
6. Ⓕ Ⓖ Ⓗ
7. Ⓐ Ⓑ Ⓒ
8. Ⓕ Ⓖ Ⓗ
9. Ⓐ Ⓑ Ⓒ
10. Ⓕ Ⓖ Ⓗ
11. Ⓐ Ⓑ Ⓒ
12. Ⓕ Ⓖ Ⓗ

Writing: Spelling
Test page: 20

Samples
- A. Ⓐ Ⓑ Ⓒ Ⓓ
- B. Ⓕ Ⓖ Ⓗ Ⓙ

Test
1. Ⓐ Ⓑ Ⓒ Ⓓ
2. Ⓕ Ⓖ Ⓗ Ⓙ
3. Ⓐ Ⓑ Ⓒ Ⓓ
4. Ⓕ Ⓖ Ⓗ Ⓙ
5. Ⓐ Ⓑ Ⓒ Ⓓ
6. Ⓕ Ⓖ Ⓗ Ⓙ
7. Ⓐ Ⓑ Ⓒ Ⓓ
8. Ⓕ Ⓖ Ⓗ Ⓙ
9. Ⓐ Ⓑ Ⓒ Ⓓ
10. Ⓕ Ⓖ Ⓗ Ⓙ

Writing: Usage
Test page: 21

Samples
- A. Ⓐ Ⓑ Ⓒ Ⓓ
- B. Ⓕ Ⓖ Ⓗ Ⓙ

Test
1. Ⓐ Ⓑ Ⓒ Ⓓ
2. Ⓕ Ⓖ Ⓗ Ⓙ
3. Ⓐ Ⓑ Ⓒ Ⓓ
4. Ⓕ Ⓖ Ⓗ Ⓙ
5. Ⓐ Ⓑ Ⓒ Ⓓ
6. Ⓕ Ⓖ Ⓗ Ⓙ
7. Ⓐ Ⓑ Ⓒ Ⓓ
8. Ⓕ Ⓖ Ⓗ Ⓙ
9. Ⓐ Ⓑ Ⓒ Ⓓ
10. Ⓕ Ⓖ Ⓗ Ⓙ

Writing: Capitalization
Test page: 22

Samples
- A. Ⓐ Ⓑ Ⓒ Ⓓ
- B. Ⓕ Ⓖ Ⓗ Ⓙ

Test
1. Ⓐ Ⓑ Ⓒ Ⓓ
2. Ⓕ Ⓖ Ⓗ Ⓙ
3. Ⓐ Ⓑ Ⓒ Ⓓ
4. Ⓕ Ⓖ Ⓗ Ⓙ
5. Ⓐ Ⓑ Ⓒ Ⓓ
6. Ⓕ Ⓖ Ⓗ Ⓙ
7. Ⓐ Ⓑ Ⓒ Ⓓ
8. Ⓕ Ⓖ Ⓗ Ⓙ

Student Answer Sheets *(cont.)*

Writing Sample
Test page: 25

Writing: Sentences
Test page: 24

Test

1. Ⓐ Ⓑ Ⓒ Ⓓ
2. Ⓕ Ⓖ Ⓗ Ⓙ
3. Ⓐ Ⓑ Ⓒ Ⓓ
4. Ⓕ Ⓖ Ⓗ Ⓙ
5. Ⓐ Ⓑ Ⓒ Ⓓ

Writing: Punctuation
Test page: 23

Sample

A. Ⓐ Ⓑ Ⓒ Ⓓ Ⓔ

Test

1. Ⓐ Ⓑ Ⓒ Ⓓ Ⓔ
2. Ⓕ Ⓖ Ⓗ Ⓙ Ⓚ
3. Ⓐ Ⓑ Ⓒ Ⓓ Ⓔ
4. Ⓕ Ⓖ Ⓗ Ⓙ Ⓚ
5. Ⓐ Ⓑ Ⓒ Ⓓ Ⓔ
6. Ⓕ Ⓖ Ⓗ Ⓙ Ⓚ
7. Ⓐ Ⓑ Ⓒ Ⓓ Ⓔ
8. Ⓕ Ⓖ Ⓗ Ⓙ Ⓚ

Student Answer Sheets (cont.)

Reading Comprehension: Figurative Language
Test page: 29

Samples

A. Ⓐ Ⓑ Ⓒ Ⓓ
B. Ⓕ Ⓖ Ⓗ Ⓙ

Test

1. Ⓐ Ⓑ Ⓒ Ⓓ
2. Ⓕ Ⓖ Ⓗ Ⓙ
3. Ⓐ Ⓑ Ⓒ Ⓓ
4. Ⓕ Ⓖ Ⓗ Ⓙ
5. Ⓐ Ⓑ Ⓒ Ⓓ
6. Ⓕ Ⓖ Ⓗ Ⓙ

Vocabulary: Synonyms and Antonyms
Test page: 28

Samples

A. Ⓐ Ⓑ Ⓒ Ⓓ
B. Ⓕ Ⓖ Ⓗ Ⓙ

Test

1. Ⓐ Ⓑ Ⓒ Ⓓ
2. Ⓕ Ⓖ Ⓗ Ⓙ
3. Ⓐ Ⓑ Ⓒ Ⓓ
4. Ⓕ Ⓖ Ⓗ Ⓙ
5. Ⓐ Ⓑ Ⓒ Ⓓ
6. Ⓕ Ⓖ Ⓗ Ⓙ
7. Ⓐ Ⓑ Ⓒ Ⓓ
8. Ⓕ Ⓖ Ⓗ Ⓙ
9. Ⓐ Ⓑ Ⓒ Ⓓ
10. Ⓕ Ⓖ Ⓗ Ⓙ

Vocabulary: Affixes
Test page: 27

Samples

A. Ⓐ Ⓑ Ⓒ Ⓓ
B. Ⓕ Ⓖ Ⓗ Ⓙ

Test

1. Ⓐ Ⓑ Ⓒ Ⓓ
2. Ⓕ Ⓖ Ⓗ Ⓙ
3. Ⓐ Ⓑ Ⓒ Ⓓ
4. Ⓕ Ⓖ Ⓗ Ⓙ
5. Ⓐ Ⓑ Ⓒ Ⓓ
6. Ⓕ Ⓖ Ⓗ Ⓙ
7. Ⓐ Ⓑ Ⓒ Ⓓ
8. Ⓕ Ⓖ Ⓗ Ⓙ

Vocabulary: Multiple Meanings
Test page: 26

Samples

A. Ⓐ Ⓑ Ⓒ Ⓓ
B. Ⓕ Ⓖ Ⓗ Ⓙ

Test

1. Ⓐ Ⓑ Ⓒ Ⓓ
2. Ⓕ Ⓖ Ⓗ Ⓙ
3. Ⓐ Ⓑ Ⓒ Ⓓ
4. Ⓕ Ⓖ Ⓗ Ⓙ
5. Ⓐ Ⓑ Ⓒ Ⓓ
6. Ⓕ Ⓖ Ⓗ Ⓙ

Student Answer Sheets *(cont.)*

Reading Comprehension: Reality Versus Fantasy
Test page: 30

Sample

A. Ⓐ Ⓑ Ⓒ Ⓓ

Test

1. Ⓐ Ⓑ Ⓒ Ⓓ
2. Ⓕ Ⓖ Ⓗ Ⓙ
3. Ⓐ Ⓑ Ⓒ Ⓓ

Reading Comprehension: Main Ideas
Test pages: 31–32

Test

1. Ⓐ Ⓑ Ⓒ Ⓓ
2. Ⓕ Ⓖ Ⓗ Ⓙ
3. Ⓐ Ⓑ Ⓒ Ⓓ
4. Ⓕ Ⓖ Ⓗ Ⓙ
5. Ⓐ Ⓑ Ⓒ Ⓓ
6. Ⓕ Ⓖ Ⓗ Ⓙ
7. Ⓐ Ⓑ Ⓒ Ⓓ

Reading Comprehension: Fiction 1
Test page: 33

Test

1. Ⓐ Ⓑ Ⓒ Ⓓ
2. _____
3. _____
4. _____
5. Ⓐ Ⓑ Ⓒ Ⓓ
6. _____

Reading Comprehension: Fiction 2
Test page: 34

Test

1. Draw picture below.
2. Ⓕ Ⓖ Ⓗ Ⓙ
3. Ⓐ Ⓑ Ⓒ Ⓓ
4. Ⓕ Ⓖ Ⓗ Ⓙ

Reading Comprehension: Fiction 3
Test page: 35

Test
1. Ⓐ Ⓑ Ⓒ Ⓓ
2. Ⓕ Ⓖ Ⓗ Ⓘ
3. Ⓐ Ⓑ Ⓒ Ⓓ
4. Ⓕ Ⓖ Ⓗ Ⓘ
5. Ⓐ Ⓑ Ⓒ Ⓓ

Reading Comprehension: Fiction 4
Test pages: 36–37

Test
1. Ⓐ Ⓑ Ⓒ Ⓓ
2. Ⓕ Ⓖ Ⓗ Ⓘ
3. Ⓐ Ⓑ Ⓒ Ⓓ
4. Ⓕ Ⓖ Ⓗ Ⓘ
5. Ⓐ Ⓑ Ⓒ Ⓓ
6. Ⓕ Ⓖ Ⓗ Ⓘ
7. Ⓐ Ⓑ Ⓒ Ⓓ
8. Ⓕ Ⓖ Ⓗ Ⓘ

Reading Comprehension: Nonfiction 1
Test pages: 38–39

Test
1. Ⓐ Ⓑ Ⓒ Ⓓ Ⓔ
2. Ⓕ Ⓖ Ⓗ Ⓘ Ⓚ
3. Ⓐ Ⓑ Ⓒ Ⓓ Ⓔ
4. Ⓕ Ⓖ Ⓗ Ⓘ Ⓚ
5. Ⓐ Ⓑ Ⓒ Ⓓ Ⓔ
6. Ⓕ Ⓖ Ⓗ Ⓘ Ⓚ
7. Ⓐ Ⓑ Ⓒ Ⓓ Ⓔ
8. Ⓕ Ⓖ Ⓗ Ⓘ Ⓚ
9. Ⓐ Ⓑ Ⓒ Ⓓ Ⓔ
10. Ⓕ Ⓖ Ⓗ Ⓘ Ⓚ

Reading Comprehension: Nonfiction 2
Test page: 40

Test
1. Ⓐ Ⓑ Ⓒ Ⓓ
2. Ⓕ Ⓖ Ⓗ Ⓘ
3. Ⓐ Ⓑ Ⓒ Ⓓ
4. Ⓕ Ⓖ Ⓗ Ⓘ
5. Ⓐ Ⓑ Ⓒ Ⓓ
6. Ⓕ Ⓖ Ⓗ Ⓘ
7. Ⓐ Ⓑ Ⓒ Ⓓ
8. Ⓕ Ⓖ Ⓗ Ⓘ

Student Answer Sheets *(cont.)*

Mathematics: Adding Like and Unlike Denominators
Test page: 48

Samples

- A. Ⓐ Ⓑ Ⓒ Ⓓ Ⓔ
- B. Ⓕ Ⓖ Ⓗ Ⓙ Ⓚ

Test

1. Ⓐ Ⓑ Ⓒ Ⓓ Ⓔ
2. Ⓕ Ⓖ Ⓗ Ⓙ Ⓚ
3. Ⓐ Ⓑ Ⓒ Ⓓ Ⓔ
4. Ⓕ Ⓖ Ⓗ Ⓙ Ⓚ
5. Ⓐ Ⓑ Ⓒ Ⓓ Ⓔ
6. Ⓕ Ⓖ Ⓗ Ⓙ Ⓚ
7. Ⓐ Ⓑ Ⓒ Ⓓ Ⓔ
8. Ⓕ Ⓖ Ⓗ Ⓙ Ⓚ
9. Ⓐ Ⓑ Ⓒ Ⓓ Ⓔ
10. Ⓕ Ⓖ Ⓗ Ⓙ Ⓚ

Mathematics: Place Value and Rounding Whole Numbers
Test page: 47

Samples

- A. Ⓐ Ⓑ Ⓒ Ⓓ
- B. Ⓕ Ⓖ Ⓗ Ⓙ

Test

1. Ⓐ Ⓑ Ⓒ Ⓓ
2. Ⓕ Ⓖ Ⓗ Ⓙ
3. Ⓐ Ⓑ Ⓒ Ⓓ
4. Ⓕ Ⓖ Ⓗ Ⓙ
5. Ⓐ Ⓑ Ⓒ Ⓓ
6. Ⓕ Ⓖ Ⓗ Ⓙ
7. Ⓐ Ⓑ Ⓒ Ⓓ
8. Ⓕ Ⓖ Ⓗ Ⓙ
9. Ⓐ Ⓑ Ⓒ Ⓓ
10. Ⓕ Ⓖ Ⓗ Ⓙ
11. Ⓐ Ⓑ Ⓒ Ⓓ
12. Ⓕ Ⓖ Ⓗ Ⓙ

Mathematics: Operations with Whole Numbers
Test pages: 45–46

Samples

- A. Ⓐ Ⓑ Ⓒ Ⓓ Ⓔ
- B. Ⓕ Ⓖ Ⓗ Ⓙ Ⓚ

Test

1. Ⓐ Ⓑ Ⓒ Ⓓ Ⓔ
2. Ⓕ Ⓖ Ⓗ Ⓙ Ⓚ
3. Ⓐ Ⓑ Ⓒ Ⓓ Ⓔ
4. Ⓕ Ⓖ Ⓗ Ⓙ Ⓚ
5. Ⓐ Ⓑ Ⓒ Ⓓ Ⓔ
6. Ⓕ Ⓖ Ⓗ Ⓙ Ⓚ
7. Ⓐ Ⓑ Ⓒ Ⓓ Ⓔ
8. Ⓕ Ⓖ Ⓗ Ⓙ Ⓚ
9. Ⓐ Ⓑ Ⓒ Ⓓ Ⓔ
10. Ⓕ Ⓖ Ⓗ Ⓙ Ⓚ
11. Ⓐ Ⓑ Ⓒ Ⓓ Ⓔ
12. Ⓕ Ⓖ Ⓗ Ⓙ Ⓚ
13. Ⓐ Ⓑ Ⓒ Ⓓ Ⓔ
14. Ⓕ Ⓖ Ⓗ Ⓙ Ⓚ
15. Ⓐ Ⓑ Ⓒ Ⓓ Ⓔ
16. Ⓕ Ⓖ Ⓗ Ⓙ Ⓚ
17. Ⓐ Ⓑ Ⓒ Ⓓ Ⓔ
18. Ⓕ Ⓖ Ⓗ Ⓙ Ⓚ
19. Ⓐ Ⓑ Ⓒ Ⓓ Ⓔ
20. Ⓕ Ⓖ Ⓗ Ⓙ Ⓚ

Research
Test pages: 41–42

Test

1. Ⓐ Ⓑ Ⓒ Ⓓ
2. Ⓕ Ⓖ Ⓗ Ⓙ
3. Ⓐ Ⓑ Ⓒ Ⓓ
4. Ⓕ Ⓖ Ⓗ Ⓙ
5. Ⓐ Ⓑ Ⓒ Ⓓ
6. Ⓕ Ⓖ Ⓗ Ⓙ
7. Ⓐ Ⓑ Ⓒ Ⓓ
8. Ⓐ Ⓑ
9. Ⓐ Ⓑ
10. Ⓐ Ⓑ
11. Ⓐ Ⓑ
12. Ⓐ Ⓑ
13. Ⓐ Ⓑ Ⓒ Ⓓ Ⓔ
14. Ⓕ Ⓖ Ⓗ Ⓙ Ⓚ
15. Ⓐ Ⓑ Ⓒ Ⓓ Ⓔ
16. Ⓕ Ⓖ Ⓗ Ⓙ Ⓚ
17. Ⓐ Ⓑ Ⓒ Ⓓ Ⓔ
18. Ⓕ Ⓖ Ⓗ Ⓙ Ⓚ

Student Answer Sheets (cont.)

Mathematics: Adding Decimals
Test page: 49

Samples

A. Ⓐ Ⓑ Ⓒ Ⓓ Ⓔ
B. Ⓕ Ⓖ Ⓗ Ⓙ Ⓚ

Test

1. Ⓐ Ⓑ Ⓒ Ⓓ Ⓔ
2. Ⓕ Ⓖ Ⓗ Ⓙ Ⓚ
3. Ⓐ Ⓑ Ⓒ Ⓓ Ⓔ
4. Ⓕ Ⓖ Ⓗ Ⓙ Ⓚ
5. Ⓐ Ⓑ Ⓒ Ⓓ Ⓔ
6. Ⓕ Ⓖ Ⓗ Ⓙ Ⓚ
7. Ⓐ Ⓑ Ⓒ Ⓓ Ⓔ
8. Ⓕ Ⓖ Ⓗ Ⓙ Ⓚ

Mathematics: Subtracting Decimals
Test page: 50

Samples

A. Ⓐ Ⓑ Ⓒ Ⓓ Ⓔ
B. Ⓕ Ⓖ Ⓗ Ⓙ Ⓚ

Test

1. Ⓐ Ⓑ Ⓒ Ⓓ Ⓔ
2. Ⓕ Ⓖ Ⓗ Ⓙ Ⓚ
3. Ⓐ Ⓑ Ⓒ Ⓓ Ⓔ
4. Ⓕ Ⓖ Ⓗ Ⓙ Ⓚ
5. Ⓐ Ⓑ Ⓒ Ⓓ Ⓔ
6. Ⓕ Ⓖ Ⓗ Ⓙ Ⓚ
7. Ⓐ Ⓑ Ⓒ Ⓓ Ⓔ
8. Ⓕ Ⓖ Ⓗ Ⓙ Ⓚ

Mathematics: Subtracting Fractions
Test page: 51

Samples

A. Ⓐ Ⓑ Ⓒ Ⓓ Ⓔ
B. Ⓕ Ⓖ Ⓗ Ⓙ Ⓚ

Test

1. Ⓐ Ⓑ Ⓒ Ⓓ Ⓔ
2. Ⓕ Ⓖ Ⓗ Ⓙ Ⓚ
3. Ⓐ Ⓑ Ⓒ Ⓓ Ⓔ
4. Ⓕ Ⓖ Ⓗ Ⓙ Ⓚ
5. Ⓐ Ⓑ Ⓒ Ⓓ Ⓔ
6. Ⓕ Ⓖ Ⓗ Ⓙ Ⓚ
7. Ⓐ Ⓑ Ⓒ Ⓓ Ⓔ
8. Ⓕ Ⓖ Ⓗ Ⓙ Ⓚ

Mathematics: Mixed Numbers
Test page: 52

Samples

A. Ⓐ Ⓑ Ⓒ Ⓓ Ⓔ
B. Ⓕ Ⓖ Ⓗ Ⓙ Ⓚ

Test

1. Ⓐ Ⓑ Ⓒ Ⓓ Ⓔ
2. Ⓕ Ⓖ Ⓗ Ⓙ Ⓚ
3. Ⓐ Ⓑ Ⓒ Ⓓ Ⓔ
4. Ⓕ Ⓖ Ⓗ Ⓙ Ⓚ
5. Ⓐ Ⓑ Ⓒ Ⓓ Ⓔ
6. Ⓕ Ⓖ Ⓗ Ⓙ Ⓚ
7. Ⓐ Ⓑ Ⓒ Ⓓ Ⓔ
8. Ⓕ Ⓖ Ⓗ Ⓙ Ⓚ

Mathematics: Problem Solving
Test pages: 53–54

Test

1. Ⓐ Ⓑ Ⓒ Ⓓ Ⓔ
2. Ⓕ Ⓖ Ⓗ Ⓙ Ⓚ
3. Ⓐ Ⓑ Ⓒ Ⓓ Ⓔ
4. Ⓕ Ⓖ Ⓗ Ⓙ Ⓚ
5. Ⓐ Ⓑ Ⓒ Ⓓ Ⓔ
6. Ⓕ Ⓖ Ⓗ Ⓙ Ⓚ
7. Ⓐ Ⓑ Ⓒ Ⓓ Ⓔ
8. Ⓕ Ⓖ Ⓗ Ⓙ Ⓚ
9. Ⓐ Ⓑ Ⓒ Ⓓ Ⓔ
10. Ⓕ Ⓖ Ⓗ Ⓙ Ⓚ

Mathematics: Customary and Metric Units
Test pages: 55–57

Test

1. Ⓐ Ⓑ Ⓒ Ⓓ
2. Ⓕ Ⓖ Ⓗ Ⓙ
3. Ⓐ Ⓑ Ⓒ Ⓓ
4. Ⓕ Ⓖ Ⓗ Ⓙ
5. Ⓐ Ⓑ Ⓒ Ⓓ
6. Ⓕ Ⓖ Ⓗ Ⓙ
7. Ⓐ Ⓑ Ⓒ Ⓓ
8. Ⓕ Ⓖ Ⓗ Ⓙ
9. Ⓐ Ⓑ Ⓒ Ⓓ
10. Ⓕ Ⓖ Ⓗ Ⓙ
11. Ⓐ Ⓑ Ⓒ Ⓓ
12. Ⓕ Ⓖ Ⓗ Ⓙ
13. Ⓐ Ⓑ Ⓒ Ⓓ
14. Ⓕ Ⓖ Ⓗ Ⓙ
15. Ⓐ Ⓑ Ⓒ Ⓓ
16. Ⓕ Ⓖ Ⓗ Ⓙ
17. Ⓐ Ⓑ Ⓒ Ⓓ
18. Ⓕ Ⓖ Ⓗ Ⓙ

Mathematics: Geometry
Test pages: 58–59

Samples

A. Ⓐ Ⓑ Ⓒ Ⓓ
B. Ⓕ Ⓖ Ⓗ Ⓙ

Test

1. Ⓐ Ⓑ Ⓒ Ⓓ
2. Ⓕ Ⓖ Ⓗ Ⓙ
3. Ⓐ Ⓑ Ⓒ Ⓓ
4. Ⓕ Ⓖ Ⓗ Ⓙ
5. Ⓐ Ⓑ Ⓒ Ⓓ
6. Ⓕ Ⓖ Ⓗ Ⓙ
7. Ⓐ Ⓑ Ⓒ Ⓓ
8. Ⓕ Ⓖ Ⓗ Ⓙ
9. Ⓐ Ⓑ Ⓒ Ⓓ
10. Ⓕ Ⓖ Ⓗ Ⓙ

Science: Plants
Test pages: 62–63

Test

1. Write comparison and contrast on back.
2. Ⓕ Ⓖ Ⓗ Ⓙ
3. Ⓐ Ⓑ Ⓒ Ⓓ
4. Ⓕ Ⓖ Ⓗ Ⓙ
5. Ⓐ Ⓑ Ⓒ Ⓓ
6. Ⓕ Ⓖ Ⓗ Ⓙ
7. Ⓐ Ⓑ Ⓒ Ⓓ
8. Ⓕ Ⓖ Ⓗ Ⓙ
9. Ⓐ Ⓑ Ⓒ Ⓓ
10. Ⓕ Ⓖ Ⓗ Ⓙ

Science: Animals
Test page: 64

Test

1. Ⓐ Ⓑ Ⓒ Ⓓ
2. Ⓕ Ⓖ Ⓗ Ⓙ
3. Ⓐ Ⓑ Ⓒ Ⓓ
4. Ⓕ Ⓖ Ⓗ Ⓙ
5. Ⓐ Ⓑ Ⓒ Ⓓ
6. Ⓕ Ⓖ Ⓗ Ⓙ
7. Ⓐ Ⓑ Ⓒ Ⓓ
8. Ⓕ Ⓖ Ⓗ Ⓙ
9. Ⓐ Ⓑ Ⓒ Ⓓ
10. Ⓕ Ⓖ Ⓗ Ⓙ

Science: Earth
Test page: 65

Test

1. Ⓐ Ⓑ Ⓒ Ⓓ
2. Ⓕ Ⓖ Ⓗ Ⓙ
3. Ⓐ Ⓑ Ⓒ Ⓓ
4. Ⓕ Ⓖ Ⓗ Ⓙ
5. Ⓐ Ⓑ Ⓒ Ⓓ
6. Ⓕ Ⓖ Ⓗ Ⓙ
7. Ⓐ Ⓑ Ⓒ Ⓓ
8. Ⓕ Ⓖ Ⓗ Ⓙ

Science: The Solar System
Test page: 66

Test

1. Ⓐ Ⓑ Ⓒ Ⓓ
2. Ⓕ Ⓖ Ⓗ Ⓙ
3. Ⓐ Ⓑ Ⓒ Ⓓ
4. Ⓕ Ⓖ Ⓗ Ⓙ
5. Ⓐ Ⓑ Ⓒ Ⓓ
6. Ⓕ Ⓖ Ⓗ Ⓙ
7. Ⓐ Ⓑ Ⓒ Ⓓ
8. Ⓕ Ⓖ Ⓗ Ⓙ
9. Ⓐ Ⓑ Ⓒ Ⓓ
10. Ⓕ Ⓖ Ⓗ Ⓙ

Science: Electricity and Magnetism
Test pages: 67–68

Test

1. Ⓐ Ⓑ Ⓒ Ⓓ
2. Ⓕ Ⓖ Ⓗ Ⓙ
3. Ⓐ Ⓑ Ⓒ Ⓓ
4. Ⓕ Ⓖ Ⓗ Ⓙ
5. Ⓐ Ⓑ Ⓒ Ⓓ
6. Ⓕ Ⓖ Ⓗ Ⓙ
7. Ⓐ Ⓑ Ⓒ Ⓓ
8. Ⓕ Ⓖ Ⓗ Ⓙ
9. Ⓐ Ⓑ Ⓒ Ⓓ
10. Ⓕ Ⓖ Ⓗ Ⓙ

Student Answer Sheets (cont.)

Science: Health and Nutrition
Test page: 69

Test

1. Ⓐ Ⓑ Ⓒ Ⓓ
2. Ⓕ Ⓖ Ⓗ Ⓙ
3. Ⓐ Ⓑ Ⓒ Ⓓ
4. Ⓕ Ⓖ Ⓗ Ⓙ
5. Ⓐ Ⓑ Ⓒ Ⓓ
6. Ⓕ Ⓖ Ⓗ Ⓙ
7. Ⓐ Ⓑ Ⓒ Ⓓ
8. Ⓕ Ⓖ Ⓗ Ⓙ
9. Ⓐ Ⓑ Ⓒ Ⓓ
10. Ⓕ Ⓖ Ⓗ Ⓙ

Social Studies: Maps and Globes
Test page: 72

Samples

A. Ⓐ Ⓑ Ⓒ Ⓓ
B. Ⓕ Ⓖ Ⓗ Ⓙ

Test

1. Ⓐ Ⓑ Ⓒ Ⓓ
2. Ⓕ Ⓖ Ⓗ Ⓙ
3. Ⓐ Ⓑ Ⓒ Ⓓ
4. Ⓕ Ⓖ Ⓗ Ⓙ
5. Ⓐ Ⓑ Ⓒ Ⓓ
6. Ⓕ Ⓖ Ⓗ Ⓙ
7. Ⓐ Ⓑ Ⓒ Ⓓ
8. Ⓕ Ⓖ Ⓗ Ⓙ
9. Ⓐ Ⓑ Ⓒ Ⓓ
10. Ⓕ Ⓖ Ⓗ Ⓙ

Social Studies: United States Regions and History 1
Test pages: 73–74

Samples

A. Ⓐ Ⓑ Ⓒ Ⓓ
B. Ⓕ Ⓖ Ⓗ Ⓙ

Test

1. Ⓐ Ⓑ Ⓒ Ⓓ
2. Ⓕ Ⓖ Ⓗ Ⓙ
3. Ⓐ Ⓑ Ⓒ Ⓓ
4. Ⓕ Ⓖ Ⓗ Ⓙ
5. Ⓐ Ⓑ Ⓒ Ⓓ
6. Ⓕ Ⓖ Ⓗ Ⓙ
7. Ⓐ Ⓑ Ⓒ Ⓓ
8. Ⓕ Ⓖ Ⓗ Ⓙ
9. Ⓐ Ⓑ Ⓒ Ⓓ
10. Ⓕ Ⓖ Ⓗ Ⓙ
11. Ⓐ Ⓑ Ⓒ Ⓓ
12. Ⓕ Ⓖ Ⓗ Ⓙ
13. Ⓐ Ⓑ Ⓒ Ⓓ
14. Ⓕ Ⓖ Ⓗ Ⓙ
15. Ⓐ Ⓑ Ⓒ Ⓓ
16. Ⓕ Ⓖ Ⓗ Ⓙ

Social Studies: United States Regions and History 2
Test pages: 75–76

Samples

A. Ⓐ Ⓑ Ⓒ Ⓓ
B. Ⓕ Ⓖ Ⓗ Ⓙ

Test

1. Ⓐ Ⓑ Ⓒ Ⓓ
2. Ⓕ Ⓖ Ⓗ Ⓙ
3. Ⓐ Ⓑ Ⓒ Ⓓ
4. Ⓕ Ⓖ Ⓗ Ⓙ
5. Ⓐ Ⓑ Ⓒ Ⓓ
6. Ⓕ Ⓖ Ⓗ Ⓙ
7. Ⓐ Ⓑ Ⓒ Ⓓ
8. Ⓕ Ⓖ Ⓗ Ⓙ
9. Ⓐ Ⓑ Ⓒ Ⓓ
10. Ⓕ Ⓖ Ⓗ Ⓙ
11. Ⓐ Ⓑ Ⓒ Ⓓ
12. Ⓕ Ⓖ Ⓗ Ⓙ
13. Ⓐ Ⓑ Ⓒ Ⓓ
14. Ⓕ Ⓖ Ⓗ Ⓙ
15. Ⓐ Ⓑ Ⓒ Ⓓ
16. Ⓕ Ⓖ Ⓗ Ⓙ

Answer Key

Writing: Syllabication — Test page: 19

Samples
- A. B
- B. (F)

Test
1.	C
2.	F
3.	B
4.	H
5.	B
6.	H
7.	A
8.	H
9.	C
10.	H
11.	B
12.	H

Writing: Spelling — Test page: 20

Samples
- A. C
- B. J

Test
1.	B
2.	F
3.	C
4.	G
5.	A
6.	G
7.	D
8.	G
9.	B
10.	J

Writing: Usage — Test page: 21

Samples
- A. B
- B. J

Test
1.	C
2.	G
3.	C
4.	G
5.	A
6.	F
7.	A
8.	J
9.	B
10.	G

Writing: Capitalization — Test page: 22

Samples
- A. C
- B. J

Test
1.	C
2.	F
3.	C
4.	G
5.	D
6.	J
7.	C
8.	J

Answer Key (cont.)

Writing: Punctuation
Test page: 23

Sample

A. C

Test

1. A
2. F
3. E
4. F
5. A
6. H
7. J
8. F

Writing: Sentences
Test page: 24

Test

1. B
2. G
3. C
4. G
5. C

Writing Sample
Test page: 25

Student responses will vary. Responses are to be evaluated by the teacher.

Answer Key *(cont.)*

Reading Comprehension: Figurative Language — Test page: 29

Samples
- A. B
- B. F

Test
1. B
2. F
3. B
4. J
5. C
6. H

Vocabulary: Synonyms and Antonyms — Test page: 28

Samples
- A. A
- B. F

Test
1. B
2. J
3. D
4. G
5. B
6. F
7. A
8. G
9. A
10. F

Vocabulary: Affixes — Test page: 27

Samples
- A. C
- B. G

Test
1. D
2. H
3. C
4. G
5. B
6. G
7. C
8. J

Vocabulary: Multiple Meanings — Test page: 26

Samples
- A. C
- B. G

Test
1. D
2. H
3. C
4. G
5. B
6. G

Answer Key (cont.)

Reading Comprehension: Reality Versus Fantasy
Test page: 30

Sample

A. Ⓐ ● Ⓒ Ⓓ

Test

1. Ⓐ Ⓑ ● Ⓓ
2. ● Ⓕ Ⓖ Ⓙ
3. Ⓐ ● ● Ⓓ

Reading Comprehension: Main Ideas
Test pages: 31–32

Test

1. Ⓐ ● Ⓒ Ⓓ
2. ● Ⓖ Ⓗ Ⓙ
3. Ⓐ Ⓑ ● ●
4. Ⓕ Ⓖ ● Ⓙ
5. Ⓐ ● Ⓒ Ⓓ
6. Ⓕ Ⓖ ● Ⓙ
7. Ⓐ ● ● Ⓓ

Reading Comprehension: Fiction 1
Test page: 33

Test

1. Ⓐ Ⓑ ● Ⓓ
2. Student responses will vary.
   Responses are to be evaluated by the teacher.
3. Student responses will vary.
   Responses are to be evaluated by the teacher.
4. Student responses will vary.
   Responses are to be evaluated by the teacher.
5. Ⓐ Ⓑ ● Ⓓ
6. Student responses will vary.
   Responses are to be evaluated by the teacher.

Reading Comprehension: Fiction 2
Test page: 34

Test

1. Drawings will vary and are to be evaluated by the teacher.
2. Ⓕ ● Ⓗ Ⓙ
3. Ⓐ Ⓑ ● Ⓓ
4. Ⓕ Ⓖ Ⓗ ●

Answer Key (cont.)

Reading Comprehension: Fiction 3
Test page: 35

Test
1. A
2. G
3. A
4. G
5. A

Reading Comprehension: Fiction 4
Test pages: 36–37

Test
1. C
2. J
3. B
4. G
5. C
6. G
7. B
8. J

Reading Comprehension: Nonfiction 1
Test pages: 38–39

Test
1. D
2. H
3. A
4. G
5. A
6. H
7. B
8. H
9. B
10. G

Reading Comprehension: Nonfiction 2
Test page: 40

Test
1. A
2. F
3. A
4. H
5. D
6. F
7. C
8. G

Research
Test pages: 41–42

Test	Answer
1.	A **B** C D
2.	**F** G H J
3.	A **B** C D
4.	F G H **J**
5.	A **B** C D
6.	F G **H** J
7.	A **B** C D
8.	A **B** C D
9.	A **B** C D
10.	**F** G H J
11.	A **B** C D
12.	**F** G H J
13.	A **B** C **D** E
14.	**F** G **H** J K
15.	A **B** C **D** E
16.	F **G** H J **K**
17.	**F**/A **B** C **D** E
18.	F **G** H J K

Mathematics: Operations with Whole Numbers
Test pages: 45–46

Samples

A.	A **B** C D
B.	F G H J **K**

Test

Test	Answer
1.	**A** B C D E
2.	F **G** H J K
3.	**A** B C D E
4.	F **G** H J K
5.	A **B** C D **E**
6.	**F** G H J **K**
7.	F **G** H J K
8.	A **B** C D E
9.	F **G** H **J** K
10.	**F** G H J K
11.	A **B** C **H** E
12.	A **B** C **J** E
13.	A **B** C **H**/D E
14.	F **G** H **J** K
15.	A **B** C **H** E
16.	F **G** H J **K**
17.	A **B** C D **E**
18.	A **B** C D E
19.	A **B** C D E
20.	**F** G H J K

Mathematics: Place Value and Rounding Whole Numbers
Test page: 47

Samples

A.	A **B** C D
B.	**F** G H J

Test

Test	Answer
1.	A **B** C D
2.	**F** G H J
3.	A **B** C D
4.	F **G** H J
5.	A **B** C D
6.	F G **H** J
7.	A B C **D**
8.	F G **H** J
9.	A B C **D**
10.	F **G** H J
11.	A **B** C D
12.	F **G** H J

Mathematics: Adding Like and Unlike Denominators
Test page: 48

Samples

A.	A B **C** D E
B.	F G **H** J K

Test

Test	Answer
1.	A B **C** D E
2.	F **G** H J K
3.	A B **C** D E
4.	F G **H** J K
5.	**A** B C D E
6.	**F** G H J K
7.	A B **C** D E
8.	**F** G H J K
9.	A B **C** D E
10.	**F** G H J K

Mathematics: Adding Decimals
Test page: 49

Samples

	Answer
A.	D
B.	J

Test

1.	E
2.	J
3.	C
4.	G
5.	C
6.	G
7.	C
8.	F

Mathematics: Subtracting Decimals
Test page: 50

Samples

	Answer
A.	A
B.	K

Test

1.	A
2.	G
3.	C
4.	G
5.	D
6.	G
7.	A
8.	G

Mathematics: Subtracting Fractions
Test page: 51

Samples

	Answer
A.	E
B.	H

Test

1.	B
2.	G
3.	D
4.	G
5.	D
6.	H
7.	A
8.	G

Mathematics: Mixed Numbers
Test page: 52

Samples

	Answer
A.	D
B.	J

Test

1.	C
2.	H
3.	C
4.	J
5.	B
6.	G
7.	E
8.	G

Science: Plants
Test pages: 62–63

Test

1. Student responses will vary. Responses are to be evaluated by the teacher.
2. C
3. G
4. H
5. G
6. F
7. F
8. G
9. G
10. ● (J)

Mathematics: Geometry
Test pages: 58–59

Samples

A. C
B. H

Test

1. C
2. H
3. C
4. H
5. C
6. F
7. A
8. F
9. H
10. F

Mathematics: Customary and Metric Units
Test pages: 55–57

Test

1. C
2. H
3. C
4. H
5. F
6. F
7. F
8. F
9. A
10. J
11. A
12. F
13. F
14. J
15. F
16. F
17. C
18. J

Mathematics: Problem Solving
Test pages: 53–54

Test

1. B
2. G
3. B
4. H
5. F
6. G
7. E
8. H
9. B
10. H

Answer Key *(cont.)*

Science: Animals
Test page: 64

Test	Answer
1.	C
2.	G
3.	D
4.	F
5.	A
6.	F
7.	C
8.	H
9.	B
10.	G

Science: Earth
Test page: 65

Test	Answer
1.	D
2.	H
3.	B
4.	G
5.	B
6.	G
7.	B
8.	J

Science: The Solar System
Test page: 66

Test	Answer
1.	B
2.	H
3.	D
4.	G
5.	B
6.	H
7.	D
8.	G
9.	B
10.	J

Science: Electricity and Magnetism
Test pages: 67–68

Test	Answer
1.	A
2.	H
3.	C
4.	G
5.	C
6.	G
7.	B
8.	G
9.	A
10.	H

Science: Health and Nutrition
Test page: 69

Test
1. B
2. H
3. B
4. G
5. D
6. F
7. B
8. J
9. A
10. J

Social Studies: Maps and Globes
Test page: 72

Samples
A. A
B. G

Test
1. C
2. G
3. C
4. G
5. B
6. J
7. D
8. G
9. B
10. J

Social Studies: United States
Regions and History 1
Test pages: 73–74

Samples
A. B
B. D

Test
1. C
2. G
3. A
4. H
5. B
6. G
7. C
8. J
9. A
10. H
11. D
12. J
13. B
14. G
15. D
16. G

Social Studies: United States
Regions and History 2
Test pages: 75–76

Samples
A. C
B. H

Test
1. B
2. F
3. A
4. J
5. B
6. F
7. C
8. H
9. C
10. J
11. B
12. F
13. B
14. G
15. D
16. H